The Smoked-Foods Recipe Book

Stackpole Books

The Smoked-Foods Recipe Book

Jack Sleight

The Smoked-Foods Recipe Book

Copyright © 1973 by
THE STACKPOLE COMPANY

Published by
Stackpole Books

Cameron and Kelker Streets, Harrisburg, Pa. 17105

Library of Congress Cataloging in Publication Data

Sleight, Jack.
    The smoked foods recipe book.

    1. Cookery (Smoked foods) I. Title.
TX835.S56   641.6'6   73-16367
ISBN 0-8117-1567-1

Printed in U.S.A.

Contents

Contents (Continued)

Equivalent Weights & Measures

3 tsp	= 1 tbsp	
4 tbsp	= 1/4 cup	
5 1/3 tbsp	= 1/3 cup	
8 tbsp	= 1/2 cup	
10 2/3 tbsp	= 2/3 cup	
12 tbsp	= 3/4 cup	
1 cup	= 1/2 pt	= 8 fluid oz
2 cups	= 1 pt	= 16 fluid oz
4 cups	= 1 qt	= 32 fluid oz
4 quarts	= 1 gal	= 128 fluid oz
8 quarts	= 1 pk	
4 pecks	= 1 bu	
2 tbsp butter	= 1 oz	
1 stick butter	= 1/2 cup	= 1/4 lb

Half a pound of most smoked meats will yield 1 cup.

One 3-lb chicken (after skin has been removed) will yield about 2 1/2 cups of diced meat.

Three lb raw shrimp, unpeeled (average 30 per lb) will yield 1 1/2 lb after smoking, or about 5 cups diced.

An 8-lb salmon (with head removed and cleaned) will weigh 7 1/2 lb after backbone, tail, and fins are removed. After smoking, it will weigh about 5 1/2 lb.

Smoking will reduce the weight of most fish at least 25 percent, and 1/2 lb smoked fish will yield about 1 cup flaked.

1 cup raw rice	= 1/2 lb or 3 cups cooked
1 cup dried beans	= 1/2 lb or 3 cups cooked
1 cup uncooked spaghetti	= 1/4 lb or 2 cups cooked
1 cup uncooked macaroni	= 1/4 lb or 2 cups cooked
1 cup uncooked noodles	= 1/4 lb or 2 cups cooked

How to Get the Most

The Smoked Foods Recipe Book is a natural follow-up to *The Home Book of Smoke-cooking Meat, Fish & Game* and is designed to fulfill the need for details on how to use and serve the basic ingredients after they emerge in their mouth-watering goodness from the smoke oven.

This book provides a wide variety of recipes using smoke-roasted foods, all of which have been tested in the author's kitchen to the delight of his many gourmet friends. Many of the recipes list alternate ingredients and, with this in mind, the user will undoubtedly try, and discover, equally delicious substitutions. For in cooking with smoked foods, improvisation becomes a practical necessity. The reader who wants to fix a certain dish may find that the meat or fish which the recipe calls for is not available, either in the ready-to-smoke or already smoked state. In such a case, the recipe can often be adapted to what is on hand. Generally, smoked rabbit or squirrel meat is a good replacement for chicken or turkey, and vice versa. And, if a favorite among these recipes is needed quickly and no smoked ingredients are on hand, any non-smoked substitute can fill in with an adjustment of the seasonings.

Chapter 4 affords the widest latitude in selecting main ingredients. Most of its recipes simply indicate fish. Salmon is the "king" of smoked fish and excels when used in these seafood recipes, but crappie, perch, sole, halibut, trout, and the variety of whitefish will also provide many tasty bites.

Keep in mind, too, that the seasonings specified by the recipes in this book are only suggestions predicated on the assumption that the smoked foods being used have been prepared with the seasonings and brines recommended in *The Home Book of Smoke-cooking Meat, Fish & Game*. If these basic, smoked-in seasonings are lighter or heavier in the smoked ingredients available, the recipe seasonings should be varied accordingly.

Here is a versatile basic seasoning which is not only excellent for smoke-roasting foods but will improve the flavor of many dishes when used in place of plain salt and pepper. It appears as an ingredient in several recipes in this book.

Basic Seasoning

1 lb 10 oz table salt
1 tbsp onion salt
2 tbsp celery salt
1 tbsp garlic salt
2 tbsp paprika
4 tbsp black pepper
4 tbsp white pepper
2 tbsp dill salt
3 tbsp monosodium glutamate
4 tbsp white sugar

Mix thoroughly; store in a covered jar in a dry place. Let it stand at least several days—the longer the better—before use.

For a spicier flavor, 1 tbsp mace and/or nutmeg may be added. For a hotter mixture, add 1 tbsp curry powder and/or dry mustard.

Flavor can also be enhanced if many of the dishes prepared are not served immediately but let stand for an hour or so, or even overnight. As ingredients are mixed together they exchange and blend flavors. This mingling also takes place as they are being heated or cooled; so preparation in advance, when possible, will add to the enjoyment.

One way to keep the dishes described in this book fresh and guard their flavor at the same time is to freeze them. The following dishes can be frozen successfully: à la king dishes, chop suey, chow mein, creamed dishes, croquettes, curried dishes, hash, all macaroni or spaghetti dishes, all soups, stews, etc., most casseroles, baked loaf dishes, and most sandwich spreads (if they do not contain mayonnaise).

Sandwiches are always popular and easily frozen. All fresh breads freeze well. Spread bread generously with soft butter to keep fillings from soaking in. Wrap finished sandwiches in moisture-vapor-proof wrapping and seal. Package sandwiches individually. For fillings, many of the Canapé Spreads and Butters in Chapter 6 are suitable. Smoked egg yolk, peanut butter, smoked chicken, turkey, meat, fish, or dried beef, and drained crushed pineapple also make good fillings. Tasty combinations are minced smoked egg yolk with sour cream and chopped dill pickle, grated smoked cheese with sour cream and chili sauce, thinly sliced smoked ham with cream cheese and chopped chives, and chopped smoked chicken with sour cream and red-pepper relish. Do not use very moist fillings, cooked egg white, or raw vegetables. For binders use lemon, orange, pineapple, or other fruit juices; milk; dairy sour cream, or applesauce. Avoid mayonnaise or salad dressing, which separate when they are frozen.

The user will get the most out of this book not only by following the foregoing suggestions but by consulting the handy guides in the back. The Recipe Locator is just what its name suggests; it lists every recipe in this book in alphabetical order opposite its page number. A Guide to Using Ingredients tells on what pages recipes using various ingredients may be found. For instance, a reader who has an abundance of eggs on hand and would like to make a dish requiring eggs need only look in this guide under Eggs to find such recipes. On the other hand, the reader who is more interested in preparing a certain type of dish than in using a certain ingredient should look under Where to Find Types of Dishes, which groups dishes according to categories: salads, soups, stews, etc.

Countless adventures in good eating await the reader who uses the recipes, suggestions, and guides in this book to create gourmet meals with smoke-roasted foods.

Bon appetit!

Chapter 1

Smoked Butcher's Meat

Casseroles and Baked Dishes

Smoked Beef Tetrazzini

1 pkg (12 oz) spaghetti
4½ qt boiling water
1/2 lb fresh mushrooms, thinly sliced
6 tbsp butter, divided
2 tbsp flour
2 cups beef bouillon or broth, heated
1 cup milk
3 tbsp dry sherry
Salt to taste
Dash nutmeg
1½ lb (3 cups) smoked beef, cut in thin
  strips
1/2 cup Parmesan cheese, grated

Gradually add spaghetti to rapidly boiling salted water so that water continues to boil. Cook, uncovered, stirring occasionally, until tender. Drain in colander. Turn into greased 2½-qt casserole. Sauté mushrooms in 3 tbsp butter until tender. In separate saucepan, melt remaining 3 tbsp butter; blend in flour. Gradually add beef bouillon and cook over medium heat, stirring constantly, until thickened. Stir in milk, sherry, salt, and nutmeg; cook over low heat 10 minutes, stirring occasionally; to sauce add spaghetti, mushrooms and smoked beef; toss lightly. Sprinkle with Parmesan cheese; bake at 350 degrees for 15 to 20 minutes or until lightly browned.

Serves 6 to 8.

Smoked Chipped Beef and Corn Casserole

1 medium onion, chopped
1/3 cup green pepper, chopped
2 tbsp butter
1/4 lb (1/2 cup) smoked beef, shredded
3 tbsp flour
2/3 cup powdered milk
1/4 tsp pepper
2 cups water
1 egg, beaten
2 cups whole kernel corn, drained
1/2 cup sharp cheddar cheese, shredded

In a saucepan sauté chopped onion and green pepper in melted butter. Add smoked beef. Cook about 5 minutes. Blend in flour. Remove from heat; add powdered milk, pepper, and water. Stir until smooth; return to heat. Cook until thickened. Blend in egg by first adding small amount of hot mixture to egg. Stir and blend back into cooked mixture. Add corn; turn into greased 2-qt casserole. Sprinkle with grated cheese. Bake in a preheated 350-degree oven for 30 minutes.

Serves 8.

Beef Casserole, Roman Style

1½ to 2 cups smoked beef, cubed
1 pkg (10 oz) frozen Italian green beans, cooked, drained
2 cups tomato sauce
1 can (4 oz) mushroom stems and pieces, drained
1/4 cup water
1 can refrigerated buttermilk or country-style biscuits
2½ slices American cheese, cut into strips 3½ x 1 inches, or 1/2 cup, grated

In ungreased 2-qt casserole combine smoked beef, green beans, tomato sauce, mushrooms and water, mixing well. Cover and bake at 350 degrees for 30 minutes until bubbly. Meanwhile, separate biscuit dough into 10 biscuits. Cut each biscuit in half and pat or roll out each half to a 4 x 1-inch strip. Cover each biscuit half with a strip of cheese or about 1 tbsp grated cheese. Starting with smallest side, roll up each biscuit strip. Place biscuits on end around top edge of hot casserole mixture and bake, uncovered, an additional 15 to 20 minutes until hot and bubbly.

Serves 6 to 8.

Scalloped Eggs

3/4 cup buttered fine bread crumbs
2 hard-cooked eggs, chopped
2 cups medium white sauce
3/4 to 1 cup smoked beef or veal

Sprinkle a greased 1½-qt casserole with half the crumbs. Cover with half the eggs, then half the sauce and half the meat. Repeat and cover with remaining crumbs. Bake at 350 degrees 20 to 30 minutes until heated through and crumbs are golden brown.

Serves 6.

Chipped Smoked Beef Casserole

1 can (10½ oz) cream of mushroom soup
1 cup milk
1 cup American cheese, grated
3 tbsp onion, minced
1 cup uncooked elbow macaroni
1 cup smoked beef, chopped
2 hard-cooked eggs, sliced

Stir soup to make a creamy consistency. Add milk, cheese, onion, uncooked macaroni, and smoked beef. Fold in eggs. Turn into greased 1½-qt baking dish. Store, covered, in refrigerator at least 3 to 4 hours or overnight. Bake 1 hour, uncovered, at 350 degrees.

Serves 4 to 6.

Oriental-Style Dishes

Smoked Beef Chop Suey

1 lb (1½ cups) smoked beef, veal,
  lean pork, or chicken
3 tbsp fat or salad oil
1 tbsp flour
1 cup hot water
2 cups onions, sliced
4 cups celery, diced
2 tbsp molasses
2 cups bean sprouts, drained
4 tbsp soy sauce
2 cups hot boiled rice

Cut meat in 1/2-inch pieces; sauté in fat, turning to brown on all sides. Add flour; mix well. Gradually add water; cook, stirring constantly, until thickened. Simmer, covered, until meat is tender. Add onions and celery; cook 10 to 15 minutes or until vegetables are tender. Add molasses, bean sprouts, and soy sauce. Cover; cook 20 minutes. Serve over boiled rice.

Serves 4 to 6.

Variations: This recipe may be varied by substituting lobster, shrimp, or duck for meat. Sautéed mushrooms, cooked diced asparagus, and whole salted almonds may be added with the molasses.

Smoked Beef Chop Suey for a Party

6 cups onions, chopped
1 cup shortening
8 cups celery, chopped
2½ qt, about 5 cans (13¾ oz ea) beef
  broth or bouillon
Basic Seasoning or salt and pepper to
  taste
4 cans (1 lb ea) Chinese vegetables,
  drained, rinsed
3/4 cup cornstarch
3/4 cup water
1/3 cup soy sauce
6 cups smoked beef, diced

Sauté onions in shortening in large saucepan just until tender. Add celery, broth, and seasonings. Bring to a boil; then cover and simmer 5 minutes. Add vegetables; bring again to a boil. Mix cornstarch, water, and soy sauce; stir into boiling mixture. Cook 1 minute or until thickened and clear. Add meat; heat thoroughly. Serve over rice.

Serves about 25.

Smoked Beef Sukiyaki

1½ lb (3 cups) smoked beef, cut in thin
  strips
3 tbsp butter or margarine
1 pkg (12 oz) long grain rice, cooked
1 can (8 oz) bamboo shoots, drained,
  cut in thin strips
2 medium onions, thinly sliced
1 can (4 oz) mushrooms, drained
1/2 cup sugar
1/2 cup dry sherry
1 cup soy sauce
Basic Seasoning or salt and pepper to
  taste
2 green onion tops, cut in 1-inch pieces
1 fresh soybean cake, cut in 1/2-inch
  squares

Lightly sauté smoked beef in butter. Stir in rice, bamboo shoots, onions, and mushrooms. Cook 10 minutes. Add sugar, sherry, soy sauce, and seasoning; mix well. Add green onion tops and soybean cubes just before serving.

Serves 4 to 6.

Creamed Dishes

Creamed Smoked Chipped Beef

1/4 lb (1 cup) smoked chipped beef
4 tbsp butter
3 tbsp flour
2 cups milk and cream
Basic Seasoning or salt and pepper to
  taste

In skillet, sauté smoked beef in butter 2 or 3 minutes until the edges curl. Stir in flour. Remove from heat and add milk and cream, stirring until smooth. Return to heat and cook about 1 minute until thickened, stirring occasionally. Season to taste and serve hot over toast, baked potatoes, or rice.

Serves 3 to 4.

Smoked Beef or Pork Julienne and Rice

A delightful dish is smoke-roasted beef or pork cut up Julienne style and served over cooked rice. Use a gravy made from beef stock. Mix meat with gravy and serve over cooked rice.

To make thin slices, partially freeze the meat before slicing. If it is thoroughly smoked or cooked, this is unnecessary.

Creamed Dried Beef

1/4 cup butter
3/4 cup smoked beef, cut up
1/4 cup green pepper, chopped
3 tbsp flour
Salt to taste
2 cups milk
1 can (4 oz) mushrooms, undrained
Corn bread, toast, or muffins

In heavy 2-qt saucepan melt butter; add beef and sauté over low heat a few minutes. Add green pepper and cook 1 minute. Stir in flour and salt until thoroughly blended. Remove from heat; gradually stir in milk; then mushrooms, including liquid. Return to heat and cook until thickened, stirring constantly. Cook 2 more minutes. Serve over corn bread, toast, or muffins.

Serves 4.

Creamed Smoked Ground Beef Dinner

1 onion, diced
2 tbsp butter
1 lb (1½ cups) smoked ground beef
2 tbsp flour
Basic Seasoning or salt and pepper to taste
1 cup milk

Sauté onion in butter in heavy skillet for 5 minutes. Add ground beef and cook until lightly sautéed. Stir in flour and seasoning. Remove from heat; gradually add milk, stirring constantly. Return to heat and cook until slightly thickened. Serve with hot biscuits for a quick dinner.

Serves 4 to 6.

Creamed Chipped Beef in Croustades

1/4 cup peanut oil
1/4 cup flour
Pepper
2 cups milk
1/2 cup smoked beef, chopped
Parsley

Pour peanut oil in top of double boiler and place over medium heat. Thoroughly blend in flour and pepper. Remove from heat. Gradually add milk, stirring until smooth. Continue cooking over boiling water until smooth and thickened, stirring constantly. Add smoked beef, cut into fairly large pieces. Serve in croustades deep-fried in peanut oil. Garnish with parsley.

Serves 3 to 4.

Corn and Smoked Beef Medley

3/4 cup smoked beef, sliced
1/4 cup butter
4 green onions, sliced
2 carrots (1 cup), peeled, shredded
3/4 cup celery, sliced
1 tsp lemon peel, grated
1½ cans (12½ oz) whole kernel corn
1/3 tbsp flour
1 cup evaporated milk
Basic Seasoning or salt and pepper to
    taste

Cut beef into bite-size pieces. Melt butter in small skillet over low heat. Add beef and onions; cook and stir until onion is tender. Stir in carrots, celery, and lemon peel. Pour half the liquid from corn into mixture. Cover and continue cooking over very low heat 5 minutes. Stir in corn; sprinkle flour over mixture, stirring until smooth. Pour in evaporated milk; cook and stir until thickened. Add seasoning to taste. Serve over toast or hot biscuits.

Serves 6.

The iridescent appearance of a piece of ham or corned beef is caused by the collection of oils from the fat on the surface of the meat.

Always carve any type of red meat roast across the grain.

There is no difference in nutrition between white and brown eggs.

When putting meat through a grinder, put several crackers through the grinder before and after grinding. This will prevent the meat from sticking to the grinder and not change the flavor of the meat.

Pasties

A pasty is a sort of Old World meat pie long popular among Cornish, Welsh, and Irish miners. It is a complete meal in a small package and is equally enjoyable warm or cold.

Savory Beef Pasties

Pasty Dough

Baking powder
2 tsp salt
4 cups flour
1 cup lard
2 tbsp butter
Water
1 egg, beaten
1 tbsp cream

Pasty Filling

1 lb (2 cups) smoked lean beef, cubed
3 raw potatoes, diced
3 green onions, diced
Basic Seasoning or salt and pepper to taste

Add a pinch of baking powder and the salt to the flour. Cut in lard and butter. Add enough cold water to make a stiff dough. Roll out about 1/8-inch thick and cut 6 circles about 6 inches in diameter. Into the center of each pastry circle put a mound of Pasty Filling ingredients (see below). Fold circle in half. Moisten around edge and crimp with a fork. Brush each with a mixture of egg and cream beaten together. Make a hole in each pasty to let steam escape. Bake at 400 degrees for 30 to 45 minutes or until browned. Serve with a side dish of brown gravy, if desired.

Mix meat, potatoes, onion, and seasoning.

Makes 6 pasties.

Smoked Beef Pub Pasties

3 cups smoked beef, chopped
1 can (10¾ oz) beef gravy, divided
1/4 cup onion, chopped
2 tsp Worcestershire sauce
Salt to taste
1 tsp prepared horseradish
2 pkg (8 oz ea) refrigerated flake-style biscuits (20)
1 egg, well beaten
2 tbsp pimiento, chopped
1/4 cup parsley, chopped

Combine beef, 1/4 cup gravy, onion, Worcestershire, salt, and horseradish; mix well. Roll out biscuits into 5-inch rounds. Divide meat mixture between 10 rounds, placing a little in the center of each. Brush edges with egg; top with remaining biscuits. Seal edges with fork. Slit tops; brush with remaining egg. Bake at 400 degrees 30 to 45 minutes or until browned. Meanwhile, in saucepan, combine remaining gravy, pimiento, and parsley. Heat, stirring occasionally. Serve with pasties.

Makes 10.

Salads

Geneva Apple Salad

2 cups smoked beef, diced
2 cups apples, cored, diced
2 cups celery, thinly sliced
1/3 cup French Dressing (see below)
6 stalks broccoli, cooked
Lettuce leaves

Mix smoked beef, apples, and celery with 1/3 cup French Dressing; chill. Pour additional French Dressing over warm cooked broccoli; cool, then chill. Place lettuce leaves on individual salad plates; arrange smoked beef mixture over lettuce. Top with marinated broccoli. Serve with additional dressing.

Serves 4 to 6.

French Dressing

1/2 cup lemon juice or vinegar
1½ cups olive oil or salad oil
Basic Seasoning or salt and pepper to taste
1/2 tsp powdered mustard
Dash cayenne pepper

Mix all ingredients together in a 1-qt jar; cover tightly and shake until thoroughly blended. Chill.

Makes 2 cups.

Smoked Beef Salad

2 cups smoked beef, diced
1 cup celery, diced
1 tbsp chives, chopped
1/2 cup mayonnaise
1 tbsp vinegar
1 tsp prepared mustard
Lettuce leaves
Parsley

Mix together smoked beef, celery and chives. Combine mayonnaise, vinegar and mustard; toss into the salad mixture. Serve on lettuce leaves and sprinkle with parsley.

Serves 4.

Scandinavian Apple Salad

1 cup smoked beef, diced
1 bunch watercress (outer leaves only), chopped
1 cup potatoes, cooked, diced
1 cup beets, cooked, diced
3 large apples, peeled, diced
2 small pickles, minced
1/4 cup capers
Tangy Dressing (see below)
Lettuce leaves
Basic Seasoning or salt and pepper to taste

Mix and thoroughly chill meat, watercress, potatoes, beets, apples, pickles, and capers. Just before serving on lettuce leaves, pour dressing over mixture and toss lightly; season to taste.

Serves 6.

Tangy Dressing

1 tsp prepared mustard
1/2 cup olive oil
Basic Seasoning or salt and pepper to taste
1/4 cup vinegar
Dash sugar
1 tbsp whipping cream

Place mustard in small bowl; gradually beat in olive oil. Add seasoning and vinegar. Add dash of sugar and whipping cream. Mix thoroughly and chill.

Generally speaking, dishes served cold need more seasoning than those served hot; heat releases the bouquet.

Mandarin Salad

1/4 cup French dressing
1 tsp soy sauce
2 cups smoked beef, diced
1 can (1 lb) bean sprouts, drained
1/4 cup onion, chopped
1/2 cup sweet pickles, chopped
Basic Seasoning or salt and pepper to taste
1/4 tsp monosodium glutamate
3/4 cup mayonnaise

Combine French dressing and soy sauce; marinate meat in mixture for 30 minutes in refrigerator. Add remaining ingredients; mix lightly. Serve on crisp salad greens.

Serves 4.

Anchovy with Smoked Beef Salad

1 cup smoked beef, diced
2 hard-cooked eggs, sliced
2 tomatoes, quartered
4 anchovies, diced
Lettuce leaves
French dressing

Combine smoked beef, eggs, tomatoes, and anchovies. Serve on lettuce with dressing.

Serves 6.

Smoked Tongue in Aspic

1 envelope unflavored gelatin
1/3 cup cold water
2 cans (10½ oz) beef bouillon
Basic Seasoning or salt and pepper to
  taste
1½ lb smoked tongue, sliced
1 can (1 lb) peas, drained
Watercress or greens

Soften gelatin in 1/3 cup cold water. Heat bouillon to boiling; add gelatin and stir until dissolved. Season to taste. Coat bottom of ring mold with one-third gelatin mixture and chill. Dip the smoked tongue slices into remaining gelatin and line the mold with overlapping slices; chill again. Add peas and pour in remaining gelatin. Chill until set. Unmold on round platter and fill center and garnish sides with watercress.

Serves 6.

Smoked Beef and Potato Salad

2 cups boiled potatoes, cooled, diced
2 cups smoked beef, diced
2 dill pickles, diced
1 apple, peeled, shredded
1 can (17 oz) peas, drained
2 hard-cooked eggs, chopped
1/2 cup mayonnaise
1/2 cup sour cream
1 tbsp prepared mustard
Basic Seasoning or salt and pepper to
  taste
1 tbsp parsley, chopped
Lettuce leaves

Mix together potatoes, smoked beef, pickles, apple, peas, and eggs. Mix the mayonnaise with sour cream and mustard. Combine half the dressing with salad mixture; season to taste. Chill for at least 2 hours. Pour remaining dressing over salad; sprinkle with parsley and serve on lettuce leaves.

Serves 8.

Sandwiches

Smoked Liver Burgers

1 cup smoked beef liver, diced
1/4 cup mayonnaise
1/2 small onion, chopped
Basic Seasoning or salt and pepper to
    taste
2 hamburger buns
2 slices American or cheddar cheese
Lettuce wedges
Pimiento strips

Combine smoked liver, mayonnaise, onion, and seasoning in a blender and mix thoroughly. Spread smoked liver mixture on bottom half of each bun; top with a slice of cheese. Broil 2 to 3 minutes along with top half of bun. Close buns to serve. Garnish with lettuce and pimiento.

Serves 2.

Hearty Smoked Meat Sandwiches

1 cup smoked beef
1/2 cup celery, minced
1 tbsp onion, grated
2 tbsp chili sauce
2 tbsp mayonnaise
8 to 10 slices bread

Combine smoked beef, celery, and onion and put through a meat grinder. Add chili sauce and mayonnaise, blending well. Spread on slices of bread and garnish with lettuce leaves.

Makes 4 or 5.

The best sandwiches are made by using firm, day-old bread rather than freshly baked bread. Rolled sandwiches, however, are better made with fresh bread with crusts removed. Wrap them in waxed paper, then a moist cloth before chilling.

Soup and Hash

Won Ton Soup

1½ cups flour
1 tsp salt
1/4 tsp monosodium glutamate
1 egg
2 tbsp water
1/2 lb (1 cup) smoked beef, chopped
Basic Seasoning or salt and pepper to
    taste
2 tsp onion, diced
4 cups chicken bouillon
1/2 cup celery, diced
1 cup fresh spinach, tightly packed

Place flour, salt, and monosodium glutamate in a mixing bowl. Stir together with one slightly beaten egg; add water. Knead on floured board until smooth. Cover and let stand 15 minutes. Roll out paper thin and cut into 3-inch squares. Chop meat very fine and combine with seasoning and onion. Place 1 tsp of mixture in center of each 3-inch square. Fold squares in half diagonally and press edges together with fork. Cook in 1 qt boiling salted water for 15 minutes. Place chicken bouillon in separate saucepan and bring to boil. Add celery and cook for 5 minutes. Clean and remove stems from spinach and add to mixture. Cook one minute. Pour over drained won ton squares in soup bowls. Serve immediately.

Serves 4.

Glorified Smoke-Roasted Hash

1 large onion, finely chopped
4 tbsp fat or salad oil
4 cups raw potatoes, cubed
4 cups smoke-roasted beef, cubed
Basic Seasoning or salt and pepper to
    taste
1/2 tsp Worcestershire sauce
2 cups hot water
3 tbsp flour
1/4 cup cold water

Sauté onion in oil until golden brown. Add potatoes, meat, seasoning, Worcestershire sauce, and hot water. Cover and cook until potatoes are tender. Mix flour and cold water to a smooth paste; add to meat-potato mixture. Heat thoroughly.

Serves 6.

Delicacies

Smoked Beef Tongue Burgundy

1 smoked beef tongue (3 to 4 lbs)
Cold water
1 onion, quartered
Celery tops
2 tbsp mixed pickling spice
1/2 cup Burgundy

Cover tongue with cold water. Add onion, celery tops, and pickling spice; cover. Bring to a boil; then reduce heat and simmer 2 hours. Add wine and cook 1 to 2 hours longer, or until tongue is tender. Remove from liquid. Cool slightly; then peel off skin and trim bone and gristle at thick end. Strain cooking liquid, reserving 2/3 cup for Wine Sauce (see below). Return to remaining liquid to keep warm until serving time, or refrigerate tongue in cooking liquid for serving cold. Slice and serve with Wine Sauce.

Serves 4 to 6.

Wine Sauce

1/2 cup currant jelly
2/3 cup Burgundy or other dry red table wine
1 tsp prepared mustard
2/3 cup cooking liquid from tongue

Break up currant jelly with fork. Add remaining ingredients and bring to a boil. Reduce heat; simmer a few minutes to develop flavor.

Makes 1½ cups sauce.

Tip: Slices of tongue may be reheated in wine sauce.

Smoked Veal Curry

2½ lbs (5 cups) smoked veal, diced
3 medium onions, minced
6 stalks celery, minced
2 apples, cored, diced
6 tbsp shortening
4 cups beef bouillon
2 tbsp curry powder
Basic Seasoning or salt and pepper to taste
1/2 tsp ginger
Few drops tabasco sauce
1/2 tsp Worcestershire sauce
1/2 cup molasses
2 egg yolks, beaten
Hot steamed rice

Sauté smoked veal, onions, celery, and apples in shortening until lightly browned; add 3½ cups bouillon. Blend together curry powder, Basic Seasoning, ginger, tabasco, Worcestershire, and 1/2 cup bouillon. Add molasses and combine with meat mixture. Cover and cook 20 minutes or until tender. Just before serving, gradually add a little hot curry gravy to egg yolks; quickly stir into meat-vegetable mixture, stirring constantly. Serve in hot seasoned rice ring. May be garnished with chutney, shredded fresh coconut, peanuts, sliced hard-cooked eggs, or chopped crisp bacon.

Serves 8.

Chapter 2

Smoke-roasted Poultry and Game Birds

Casseroles and Baked Dishes

Smoked Chicken and Vegetable Casserole

1/2 cup milk
1/2 cup mayonnaise
Basic Seasoning or salt and pepper to
    taste
2 cups cooked vegetables, minced
1 cup smoked chicken, chopped
1/4 tsp celery salt
1/3 cup fine dry bread crumbs
1 tbsp melted butter

Gradually stir milk into mayonnaise in saucepan. Add seasoning. Cook over low heat, stirring constantly, until hot. Add vegetables, chicken, celery salt. Heat gently. Pour into a greased 1-qt casserole. Combine bread crumbs and butter. Sprinkle over top of chicken-vegetable mixture. Broil 4 inches from source of heat about 2 minutes or until crumbs are browned.

Serves 4 to 5.

Smoked Chicken and Noodle Casserole

1/4 cup onion, chopped
1/4 cup green pepper, chopped
2 tbsp butter or margarine
2 cups smoked chicken, diced
1 pkg (8 oz) noodles, cooked and drained
1 tbsp lemon juice
1/2 cup mayonnaise
1/3 cup milk
1 medium tomato, peeled and cut up
Basic Seasoning or salt and pepper to
    taste
1/2 cup cheese, shredded

Sauté onion and green pepper in butter about 5 minutes. Combine with remaining ingredients, except cheese. Turn into 2-qt casserole. Top with cheese. Bake in 350-degree oven about 20 minutes or until heated through.

Serves 6.

Curried Smoked Chicken Salad Casserole

2 cups smoked chicken, diced
2 cups celery, diced
1 tsp curry powder
1 cup mayonnaise
Basic Seasoning or salt and pepper to
    taste
1/4 cup almonds, slivered

Mix together smoked chicken, celery, curry powder, and mayonnaise. Season to taste. Put into 4 individual greased casseroles. Sprinkle with almonds. Bake in a 350-degree oven 20 to 25 minutes.

Serves 4.

Smoked Chicken Almandine

3 tbsp butter or margarine, divided
2 tbsp flour
1 cup milk, scalded
Basic Seasoning or salt and pepper to
 taste
1 tsp onion, minced
1/2 cup dry white wine
1 cup chicken broth
1 clove
1 small bay leaf
3½ to 4 cups smoked chicken, diced
1/2 cup toasted almonds, slivered
3 egg yolks
1/4 cup whipping cream
1/4 cup dry sherry
1 tbsp Angostura bitters
2 tbsp bread or cornflakes crumbs

Make white sauce by melting in skillet 2 tbsp butter; blend in flour. Gradually add milk, stirring until smooth and thickened. Season to taste. Lightly sauté onion in 1/2 tbsp butter. Stir in white sauce, dry white wine, chicken broth, clove, and bay leaf. Simmer about 5 minutes; stir in chicken and almonds. Mix together egg yolks, cream, sherry, and bitters, blending well; stir into chicken mixture and pour into greased 10-inch casserole. Melt remaining 1/2 tbsp butter, stirring in the crumbs; sprinkle over casserole mixture. Bake 15 minutes in a 350-degree oven, uncovered. Brown under broiler.

Serves 10.

Smoked Turkey or Chicken Almandine

5 tbsp butter or margarine, divided
4 tbsp flour
2 cups milk
2 tbsp dry white wine
2 cups smoked turkey, diced
1 cup cooked peas
1/3 cup toasted almonds, slivered
2 egg yolks
Salt to taste
2 tbsp bread or cornflake crumbs
2 tbsp Parmesan cheese, grated

In skillet melt 4 tbsp butter; stir in flour. Remove from heat and blend in milk, stirring until smooth and thickened. Return to heat and add wine, stirring until sauce is smooth. Stir in turkey, peas, and half the almonds. Lightly beat the egg yolks with a fork, adding a little sauce, and rapidly stir back into the turkey mixture. Season to taste. Pour mixture into a small greased casserole. Scatter remaining almonds on top, then crumbs, 1 tbsp butter, and finally the Parmesan cheese. Bake 45 minutes in 375-degree oven. Brown under broiler.

Serves 4.

Smoked Chicken or Turkey and Rice Curry

1 stick (¼ lb) butter or margarine
4 tbsp flour
2½ cups milk, heated
1/2 cup cream or canned milk, heated
Basic Seasoning or salt and pepper to taste
2 cups smoked chicken, cubed
2 tsp curry powder
1/4 cup dry sherry
2 cups cooked rice
1 tbsp parsley, minced
Parmesan cheese, grated

Melt half the butter in saucepan; blend in flour and gradually stir in heated milk and cream. Season to taste. Melt remaining butter in 8-inch skillet and lightly sauté the smoked chicken cubes. Stir in cream sauce, curry powder, and sherry. Heat through; stir in rice and parsley. Top with cheese and brown under broiler.

Serves 6.

Smoked Turkey with Wild Rice

1 cup raw wild rice
2 cups smoked turkey, diced
1/2 lb mushrooms, sliced
1½ cups whipping cream
2 tsp chives or green onion, chopped
2½ cups chicken broth bouillon, divided
Basic Seasoning or salt and pepper to taste
Grated cheese
Butter

Wash rice in several waters and let soak in cool water for about 2 hours. Drain well and mix with turkey, mushrooms, cream, chives, and 1½ cups broth; season to taste. Bake, covered, in greased 2-qt casserole at 350 degrees for 1 hour. Stir in the remaining broth and bake another 30 minutes or until the broth is absorbed and, when stirred with a fork, the rice is fluffy and tender. Sprinkle with cheese; dot with butter. Place, uncovered, under broiler until golden brown.

Serves 6.

Smoked Chicken with Nuts and Spaghetti

1 can (10½ oz) cream of mushroom soup
1 can (10½ oz) cream of chicken soup
1/2 cup Swiss or sharp cheddar cheese, grated
3/4 cup light cream or evaporated milk
1 pkg (16 oz) thin spaghetti, cooked, cooled
1/2 cup almonds or Brazil nuts, slivered
1 pimiento, thinly sliced
2 cups smoked chicken or turkey, diced
Paprika

Stir together the soups, cheese, and cream; cook over medium heat until warm. Add spaghetti, nuts, pimiento, and smoked chicken. Pour into a greased 8-inch casserole; sprinkle with paprika. Bake in a 325-degree oven about 20 minutes.

Serves 6.

Smoked Turkey-Spaghetti Casserole

2 cups smoked turkey, diced
Pimiento, chopped
1/2 medium onion, chopped
1/4 green pepper, chopped
1 can (10½ oz) cream of mushroom soup
1/2 cup dry white wine
1½ cups cooked spaghetti
Basic Seasoning or salt and pepper to taste
3/4 cup sharp cheddar cheese, grated

In greased 2½-qt casserole mix smoked turkey, pimiento, onion, and green pepper. In a separate pan, heat soup and wine; stir in spaghetti and pour into casserole, blending the two mixtures. Season to taste. Sprinkle with cheese. Bake in a 350-degree oven about 45 minutes or until heated through.

Serves 6.

Smoked Chicken and Macaroni Casserole

3 cups macaroni, cooked (1½ cups uncooked)
2 cups cheddar cheese, grated
1½ cups smoked chicken, chopped
1/2 cup bread crumbs
1 cup mushrooms, sliced
1/4 cup pimiento, chopped
1 can (10½ oz) cream of chicken soup plus milk enough to make 2 cups

Mix together all ingredients. Pour into greased 4-qt baking dish. Bake 1 hour in preheated 350-degree oven.

Serves 6 to 8.

Smoked Chicken or Turkey Divan with Nuts

6 tbsp butter or margarine
6 tbsp flour
3 cups milk, scalded
3 egg yolks, slightly beaten
Salt to taste
1/4 tsp tabasco sauce
4 tbsp Parmesan cheese, grated
12 sprouts cooked broccoli
1/2 cup toasted Brazil nuts or almonds, sliced
6 or 8 smoked chicken slices

In skillet melt butter; blend in flour. Gradually add milk, stirring until smooth and thickened. Add a little sauce to egg yolks and blend back into the cream sauce. Cook 1 or 2 minutes, but do not boil. Season to taste. Stir in tabasco and cheese. Arrange cooked broccoli on bottom of greased casserole. Add a thin layer of cream sauce and sprinkle with half the nuts. Top with a thick layer of smoked chicken slices, overlapping them. Cover with remaining sauce. Bake 20 minutes in a 375-degree oven. Sprinkle with remaining nuts and bake 5 minutes longer. Brown under the broiler for a minute.

Serves 6.

Baked Smoked Chicken Salad

2 cups elbow macaroni
4 cups smoked chicken, diced
1/3 cup toasted almonds, chopped
1 tbsp lemon juice
1 tsp grated lemon rind
1½ cups Swiss cheese, grated
Basic Seasoning or salt and pepper to taste
1½ cups mayonnaise
Parsley

Cook and drain macaroni. Combine with remaining ingredients, except parsley. Turn into buttered 2-qt baking dish. Bake in 350-degree oven 30 minutes. Garnish with parsley.

Serves 4 to 6.

Smoked Chicken Tamale Pie

2 to 3 cups Cornmeal Mush (see below)
2 to 3 cups smoked chicken, sliced
Basic Seasoning or salt and pepper to taste
1 can (8 oz) tomato sauce
1 can (1 lb) whole kernel corn, drained
2 tbsp sugar
2 tbsp olive oil
1/2 cup raisins, scalded, chopped
10 ripe olives, sliced
3/4 cup Parmesan cheese, grated

Spread cornmeal mush in bottom of greased shallow casserole. Arrange smoked chicken over the mush; sprinkle with seasoning. Combine remaining ingredients, except cheese, to make a sauce, adding more seasoning if desired. Pour over chicken and sprinkle cheese over top. Bake in 350-degree oven 45 minutes.

Serves 6 to 8.

Cornmeal Mush

For 3 cups of cornmeal mush, cook 1/2 cup dry cornmeal in 3 cups boiling water with 1¼ tsp salt.

Smoked Chicken and Potato Florentine

1 pkg instant mashed potato granules
1 pkg (10 oz) frozen spinach, thawed, chopped
4 eggs, separated
1 cup smoked chicken, chopped
1/8 tsp cayenne pepper
1/4 cup cheddar cheese, grated

Prepare mashed potatoes as directed on package; stir in spinach, smoked chicken, pepper, and lightly beaten egg yolks; mix thoroughly. Beat egg whites until stiff peaks form; fold into potato mixture. Turn into ungreased 1½-qt casserole. Sprinkle with cheese and bake in preheated 350-degree oven for about 1 hour, until puffed and golden.

Serves 6.

Smoked Turkey or Chicken for a Party

3/4 cup butter, margarine or salad oil, divided
3/4 cup cooked ham cut in julienne strips
1/2 lb mushrooms, sliced
1 pkg (16 oz) spaghetti, cooked
1/2 cup Parmesan cheese, grated, divided
2 tbsp whipping cream
6 tbsp dry sherry, divided
1½ cups whipping cream, whipped to make 3 cups
2 tsp paprika
3 cups medium white cream sauce
2 egg yolks, lightly beaten
1 qt smoked turkey, cubed
Basic Seasoning or salt and pepper to taste

Heat 1/4 cup butter in a large skillet and sauté the ham and mushrooms about 5 minutes or until mushrooms are tender, stirring occasionally. Drain cooked spaghetti and toss with 1/4 cup butter, 1/4 cup grated cheese, 2 tbsp cream, and 2 tbsp sherry. Spread spaghetti in bottom of greased 2-qt casserole. Stir whipped cream and paprika into cream sauce; heat almost to boiling. Stir about 1/2 cup sauce into egg yolks; stir quickly back into the sauce. Mix in the ham-mushroom mixture and smoked turkey. Heat well, stirring in 4 tbsp sherry. Season to taste. Gently pour mixture over spaghetti. Dribble remaining 1/4 cup melted butter on top and sprinkle with remaining cheese. Bake 25 to 30 minutes in a 350-degree oven. Brown quickly under broiler.

Serves 12.

Smoked Chicken and Spaghetti

3 tbsp olive or salad oil
1 medium onion, minced
1 small green pepper, minced
2 cans (8 oz) tomato sauce
1 cup mushrooms, sliced
Basic Seasoning or salt and pepper to taste
1/2 tsp oregano
1 pkg (16 oz) spaghetti, cooked
3 cups smoked chicken, diced
1 cup mozzarella cheese, grated

In skillet heat oil; sauté onion and green pepper until the onions begin to brown. Stir in tomato sauce, mushrooms, and seasonings; cover and simmer, stirring frequently, over low heat for about 25 to 30 minutes. Correct seasoning to taste. In greased 2½-qt casserole, alternate layers of spaghetti, smoked chicken, and cheese, smothering each layer with sauce and ending with cheese. Bake in a 350-degree oven about 30 minutes.

Serves 8.

To avoid cheese becoming stringy, do not cook at a high temperature.

Smoked Chicken with Saffron Rice

2½ cups smoked chicken, chopped
3 medium onions, minced
1 small clove garlic, minced
1/4 lb ham, diced
2 tsp olive oil
1 cup uncooked rice
1/4 tsp powdered saffron
1 bay leaf
1 can (16 oz) tomatoes
1 can (4 oz) pimiento, drained, sliced
1 cup water
6 sprigs parsley, minced
Basic Seasoning or salt and pepper to taste
Stuffed olives

Place smoked chicken in greased 4-qt casserole. Sauté onion, garlic, and ham in oil in skillet until onions are transparent. Cook rice according to package directions with saffron; drain and add to skillet with remaining ingredients, except olives. Pour over smoked chicken. Cover; bake at 350 degrees for 30 to 45 minutes. Garnish with olives.

Serves 6 to 8.

Smoked Turkey and Lemon Rice Casserole

2 cups cooked rice
3 cups smoked turkey, chopped
Basic Seasoning or salt and pepper to taste
1/2 tsp whole celery seed
1 can (8 oz) tomato sauce
1 cup chicken broth or bouillon
4 lemon slices
5 thin onion slices
1/3 cup dry white wine
2 tbsp butter
1 tsp paprika

Spread the cooked rice in a greased 2½-qt casserole and evenly arrange the turkey over it. Sprinkle with seasoning and celery seed. Mix well tomato sauce and chicken broth; pour over turkey. Cut lemon and onion slices in half and arrange over casserole mixture, adding more if needed. Bake, covered, 1 hour in a 350-degree oven. Check halfway through and add a little broth if it seems too dry. When done, uncover and add wine. Dot with butter cut in bits; sprinkle with paprika and broil until golden brown.

Serves 6.

Smoked Chicken Chow Bake

2 cups smoked chicken, diced
1 can (10½ oz) cream of mushroom soup
1 cup pineapple tidbits
1 tbsp soy sauce
1 cup celery, sliced
2 tbsp green onions, sliced
2½ cups chow mein noodles

Combine all ingredients, except noodles, mixing well. Gently fold in 1 cup noodles. Turn into 8 x 8 x 2-inch baking dish. Top with remaining noodles. Bake in 350-degree oven 30 minutes or until hot. Serve with additional soy sauce.

Serves 4 to 5.

*Creamed Dried
Smoked Beef*

*Smoked Turkey
and Spaghetti Casserole*

Smoked Salmon Fruit Salad

Spaghetti au Diable

1 pkg (8 oz) spaghetti
1 onion, diced
1 small clove garlic
2 tbsp fat
2½ cups cooked tomatoes
Basic Seasoning or salt and pepper to taste
1 tbsp sugar
Dash cayenne
1/2 cup smoked chicken, diced
1 cup mushrooms, sautéed
Grated cheese

Cook spaghetti in boiling salted water until tender; drain and place in greased casserole. Sauté onion and garlic in fat until tender but not brown. Add tomatoes, seasoning, sugar, and cayenne. Heat to boiling; add smoked chicken and mushrooms; pour over spaghetti. Toss with a fork. Sprinkle with grated cheese and bake in 350-degree oven until mixture is heated through and cheese is melted.

Serves 6 to 8.

Chicken or Turkey Tetrazzini

1 pkg (8 oz) spaghetti, uncooked
1/2 cup mushrooms, sliced
3 tbsp butter
3 tbsp flour
1 cup turkey broth or canned consommé
3/4 cup dry white wine or milk
1/2 cup cream or evaporated milk
Basic Seasoning or salt and pepper to taste
1½ cups smoked turkey or chicken, diced
1/2 cup fine dry bread crumbs
1/4 cup Parmesan cheese, grated

Cook spaghetti according to package directions; drain. Sauté mushrooms in butter for 5 minutes. Blend in flour; then stir in heated broth and wine. Cook until smooth, stirring constantly. Add cream and seasoning to taste. In greased baking dish, alternate layers of spaghetti, diced smoked turkey, and mushroom sauce. Repeat, ending with a thin layer of spaghetti. Sprinkle with crumbs mixed with grated cheese; dot with butter and bake at 350 degrees for 30 minutes.

Serves 6.

Smoked Chicken Yorkshire

2 cups smoked chicken, diced
2 eggs
1/2 cup fat, melted
1 cup milk
1 cup flour, sifted
1 tsp baking powder
1/2 tsp salt
Leftover gravy

Place smoked chicken in bottom of greased casserole and set in oven to heat. Beat eggs, fat, and milk together. Sift dry ingredients together; add to liquid ingredients and beat until smooth. Batter will be quite thin. Pour over smoked chicken and bake in 350-degree oven 30 minutes. Serve at once with gravy.

Serves 6.

Ground Smoked Turkey or Chicken Loaf

4 tsp powdered chicken broth or 2
   chicken bouillon cubes
1 cup boiling water
2 eggs, beaten
1/3 cup onion, chopped
3/4 cup powdered milk
3 cups soft bread crumbs
1/2 tsp fine herbs
Basic Seasoning or salt and pepper to taste
4 cups ground smoked turkey or chicken

Dissolve powdered chicken broth in boiling water; cool. Add eggs and onion. In large bowl combine powdered milk, bread crumbs, and seasonings. Add bouillon mixture and stir well with wooden spoon. Add ground turkey and mix well. Shape into greased 10 x 6-inch loaf pan. Bake in preheated 350-degree oven about 1 hour.

Serves 8 to 10.

Quick and Tasty Smoked Chicken Casserole

1½ cups medium white sauce
2 hard-cooked eggs, chopped
1 tbsp lemon juice
1 cup smoked chicken, diced
Basic Seasoning or salt and pepper to
   taste
2 tsp onion, finely chopped
1 cup celery, sliced
1/2 cup almonds, chopped
Bread crumbs

Combine all ingredients, except bread crumbs. Pour into greased 1½-qt casserole. Top with bread crumbs and bake in a preheated 350-degree oven for 30 minutes or until bubbly.

Serves 4.

Country Smoked Chicken Loaf

2 cups smoked chicken, diced
1/2 cup carrots, cooked, chopped
1 cup peas, cooked
1/2 cup celery, chopped
1 tbsp green pepper, minced
1 cup bread crumbs
1/2 cup milk
2 egg yolks, beaten
1 tsp onion juice
1 tsp lemon juice
Basic Seasoning or salt and pepper to
   taste

Mix all ingredients thoroughly and place in greased 9 x 5-inch loaf pan or ring mold. Bake in 350-degree oven until firm, about 40 minutes. Garnish with celery, carrot and bread sticks, and lemon slices or serve with a cream or mushroom sauce.

Serves 6.

Variation: Omit carrots and lemon juice. Use 2 cups whole peas and 1½ cups smoked chicken instead of above amounts. Use 2 cups cooked rice instead of bread crumbs. Use diced pimiento instead of green pepper.

Smoked Chicken and Lobster Casserole

3 tbsp butter or margarine
3 tbsp flour
2 cups chicken broth or bouillon, or equal
    amounts broth and dry white wine
Basic Seasoning or salt and pepper to taste
2 egg yolks
1/2 cup whipping cream, divided
1/2 cup mushrooms, sliced
1 cup cooked peas
1/2 lb lobster, cooked, diced
6 medium slices smoked chicken
Cheddar cheese, grated
Paprika

Melt butter in saucepan. Stir in flour, slowly blending in heated chicken broth and stirring until smooth and thickened. Season to taste; remove from heat. Lightly beat together egg yolks and 1/4 cup cream; stir into sauce. Add mushrooms, peas, and lobster. Whip remaining 1/4 cup cream and fold into sauce. Layer smoked chicken slices in greased 1½-qt casserole; pour lobster sauce over chicken. Sprinkle with cheese and paprika. Bake about 15 minutes in a 325-degree oven until golden brown.

Serves 4.

Smoked Turkey and Rice Casserole with Olives

1/4 cup butter or margarine
1½ cups smoked turkey
1/3 cup Spanish olives, sliced
1 cup turkey or chicken stock or bouillon
1/2 cup milk
Basic Seasoning or salt and pepper to taste
2 cups cooked rice
3/4 cup cheddar cheese, grated

In saucepan melt butter; add turkey, olives, stock, milk, and seasoning; mix well and bring to boil. Arrange rice in 4 greased individual baking dishes. Top with olive mixture and sprinkle with cheese. Bake at 350 degrees 30 minutes or until heated through.

Serves 4.

Smoked Duck Casserole Supreme

2½ cups uncooked broad noodles, broken
4 tbsp shortening
4 tbsp flour
Basic Seasoning or salt and pepper to
    taste
2 cups milk, scalded
1 tbsp onion, grated
1½ cups American cheese, grated, divided
2 cups smoked duck, chopped
3 tbsp pimiento, chopped
3 tbsp parsley, chopped

Cook noodles according to package directions until tender. Melt shortening in saucepan; add flour and seasoning, blending well. Gradually stir in milk; add grated onion and cook over low heat, stirring until thickened. Add 1 cup grated cheese and stir until cheese is melted. Mix in cooked noodles, duck, pimiento, and parsley. Turn into greased 2-qt casserole. Sprinkle remaining grated cheese over top. Bake at 350 degrees for 45 to 50 minutes until bubbly and browned.

Serves 6.

Chinese Chicken Casserole

2 tbsp salad oil
1/2 onion, sliced
1/2 cup mushrooms, sliced
1 cup celery, sliced
1 can (8½ oz) water chestnuts
1 cup chicken broth
1½ cups smoked chicken, chopped
1 tsp cornstarch
Salt to taste
2 tbsp water
1 tbsp soy sauce
1 can (16 oz) bean sprouts, drained
1/2 cup almonds, toasted, blanched,
    slivered
3 cups cooked rice

Heat oil in large skillet or electric fry pan. Lightly sauté onion, mushrooms, celery, and water chestnuts for about 5 minutes. Pour into greased 1½-qt casserole. Add chicken broth and smoked chicken. Bake, uncovered, about 15 minutes in a 350-degree oven. Blend together the cornstarch, salt, water, and soy sauce; stir into casserole mixture. Bake another 10 minutes. Stir in bean sprouts and almonds; heat well in oven, about 5 minutes. Serve immediately over hot fluffy rice.

Serves 5 to 6.

Escalloped Smoked Turkey and Cauliflower

1 head cauliflower
3 tbsp fat
Basic Seasoning or salt and pepper to
    taste
3 tbsp flour
1½ cups turkey stock or milk, heated
2 cups smoked turkey, diced

Break cauliflower into flowerets and cook in boiling salted water about 6 minutes, or until almost tender; drain. Melt fat and add seasoning and flour. Add stock and cook until thickened, stirring constantly. Arrange cauliflower and turkey in greased casserole; add sauce and bake in 350-degree oven until heated through, about 20 minutes.

Serves 4 to 6.

Smoked Chicken and Noodle Casserole with Mushrooms

1 cup smoked chicken or turkey, diced
3/4 lb mushrooms, sliced
1/2 green pepper, diced
1 pkg (8 oz) noodles, cooked
1/2 cup grated Swiss or sharp
    cheddar cheese
2 cups medium white sauce
Basic Seasoning or salt and pepper to
    taste
Chopped parsley

Mix all ingredients, except parsley, in a greased 8-inch casserole. Season to taste. Cover and bake 1 hour at 325 degrees. After the first 30 minutes, remove the cover. Sprinkle with parsley before serving.

Serves 6.

Try to have something chewy in all casseroles.

Smoked Pheasant and Rice Almandine

1½ cups raw rice (4½ cups cooked)

3 cups chicken broth or half dry white wine and half broth

1 tsp saffron

1 can black Bing cherries, pitted

1/4 cup white raisins

1/4 cup slivered almonds, or 1/2 cup whole

1/2 tsp dried rosemary or 1½ tsp fresh, chopped

1/2 tsp dill or dill weed

1/2 cup salad oil

4 small white onions, sliced

2 cups smoked pheasant, diced

Basic Seasoning or salt and pepper to taste

1 tbsp parsley, chopped

Mix together uncooked rice, chicken broth, and saffron in top of double boiler and cook, covered, over boiling water, without stirring, 30 to 35 minutes or until flaky and liquid is absorbed. Stir in cherries, raisins, almonds, and herbs. Heat oil in heavy skillet and lightly brown the onions. Stir in pheasant; continue cooking 1 or 2 minutes and add the rice mixture. Correct seasonings and bake, covered, in a 350-degree oven about 20 minutes. Sprinkle with parsley before serving.

Serves 6 to 8.

Smoked Goose Elegante

1/4 cup butter or margarine

1/4 cup flour

1 can (10½ oz) cream of chicken soup

1/4 cup blue cheese, crumbled

1/2 tsp dried or 1½ tsp fresh marjoram

1/2 cup Parmesan cheese, grated, divided

2 cups smoked goose, diced

1 pkg (10 oz) frozen broccoli, cooked, chopped

1 cup sour cream

Basic Seasoning or salt and pepper to taste

1/4 cup bread or cornflake crumbs

Paprika

Melt butter in large saucepan; stir in flour and remove from heat. Gradually stir in soup, blue cheese, marjoram, 1/4 cup Parmesan, goose, and broccoli. Heat just to boiling; remove from heat and stir in sour cream. Season to taste. Pour into greased 2-qt casserole and top with remaining Parmesan mixed with bread crumbs. Sprinkle with paprika. Bake in a 350-degree oven 20 minutes or until golden brown and bubbly.

Serves 6.

For a different flavor for many casserole dishes, grease the inside of a baking dish with garlic spread.

Smoked Duck Almandine

2 tbsp butter or margarine
2 tbsp flour
Basic Seasoning or salt and pepper to
  taste
1/4 tsp prepared mustard
2 cups milk, scalded
1 cup sharp cheddar cheese, grated
1 pkg (10 oz) frozen broccoli, cooked
2 cups noodles, cooked
2 cups smoked duck, chopped
1/3 cup toasted almonds, slivered

Make a cream sauce by melting butter in skillet, blending in flour, seasoning, and mustard, and gradually adding the milk. Stir constantly until smooth and thickened. Add cheese and stir until melted. Cut off broccoli stems and chop. Spread stems in shallow greased casserole; cover with noodles and then add smoked duck. Pour cheese sauce over casserole and scatter broccoli flowerets on top, pressing them lightly into sauce. Sprinkle with almonds. Bake in a 350-degree oven 15 minutes or until bubbly or heated through.

Serves 4 to 5.

Smoked Chicken Ring or Loaf

2 cups milk, heated, or stock and cream
2 eggs or 3 egg yolks, slightly beaten
1 cup soft bread crumbs
1/2 tsp salt
1/4 tsp paprika
1 tsp Worcestershire sauce
3 cups smoked chicken, diced
1/2 cup celery, chopped
1 green pepper, chopped
1½ tbsp lemon juice

Pour hot milk slowly onto eggs, stirring constantly. Add remaining ingredients; mix well and pour into buttered ring or loaf mold. Bake in 300-degree oven until knife inserted in center comes out clean, about 45 to 60 minutes. Let stand 10 minutes before unmolding. Serve mushroom sauce in center of ring.

Serves 6 to 8.

Variation: Omit milk, lemon juice, and Worcestershire sauce. Use only 3 tbsp crumbs. Add 3 tbsp diced pimiento, 1½ tsp minced onion, and 3/4 cup each tomato juice and cooked rice. Pour into mold packed with 3/4-inch layer of cooked rice and bake.

Smoked Chicken and Mushrooms in Sour Cream Sauce

2 cups smoked chicken, chopped
Basic Seasoning or salt and pepper to
  taste
1 lb mushrooms, sliced
2 tbsp butter or margarine
2 cups sour cream
Paprika

Put chicken in greased 1½-qt casserole and sprinkle with seasoning. Brown mushrooms in butter in skillet until tender. Sprinkle over chicken and season. Bake in 350-degree oven until smoked chicken is heated through. Remove from oven and mix in sour cream. Cover and bake about 10 minutes longer. Sprinkle with paprika and serve.

Serves 4.

Smoked Chicken Jambalaya

1½ cups smoked chicken, diced
1 cup rice, cooked
1½ cups tomatoes, cooked
1 large onion, chopped
1/2 green pepper, chopped
1/2 cup celery, chopped
Basic Seasoning or salt and pepper to
    taste
Buttered crumbs

Combine chicken, rice, and tomatoes; cook for 10 minutes. Add onion, green pepper, celery, and seasoning. Turn into baking dish and cover with buttered crumbs. Bake in 350-degree oven for 1 hour.

Serves 4.

Hot Smoked Turkey Salad

2 cups smoked turkey, diced
2 cups celery, thinly sliced
1 tsp onion, grated
Salt to taste
1/2 cup water chestnuts, sliced
3/4 cup mayonnaise
2 tbsp lemon juice
1 cup corn chips, crushed
1/2 cup sharp cheddar cheese, grated

Combine all ingredients, except corn chips and cheese. Pile into shallow 1½-qt baking dish or 4 to 6 individual ramekins. Sprinkle with corn chips and cheese. Bake in 450-degree oven 10 to 15 minutes.

Serves 4 to 6.

Oriental-Style Dishes

Smoked Chicken Chop Suey

2 tbsp fat
3/4 cup onion, thinly sliced
1 cup celery, thinly sliced
2 cups cabbage, thinly shredded
1/2 tsp salt
3 cups smoked chicken, thinly shredded
1/4 cup soy sauce
1/2 cup chicken stock

Heat fat in heavy skillet; sauté onion until lightly browned. Add celery, cabbage, and salt; cook 5 minutes. Add smoked chicken, soy sauce, and stock. Cook over low heat, covered, until vegetables are tender, about 15 minutes. If the liquid needs thickening use cornstarch or flour blended with a little cold water.

Serves 6.

Smoked Turkey Mandarin

Cream Puffs

    1 cup water
    1/2 cup butter
    1 cup flour
    1/2 tsp salt
    4 eggs

Mandarin Filling

    2 tbsp butter
    1 cup almonds, slivered
    2 cups smoked turkey, diced
    1 can (1 lb) sweet and sour sauce
    1 tbsp lemon juice
    Salt to taste
    1 can (8½ oz) water chestnuts, drained
        and coarsely chopped
    1/3 cup green onions, sliced
    1 can (4 oz) mushrooms, drained, sliced
    1 can (11 oz) mandarin oranges, drained

In saucepan bring water and butter to a boil, stirring until butter melts. Add flour and salt all at once. Reduce heat. Cook, vigorously stirring until mixture is smooth and forms soft ball, 1 to 2 minutes. Remove from heat and cool slightly. Add eggs, one at a time, beating well after each addition. Drop batter by rounded tablespoonfuls onto greased baking sheet. Bake at 400 degrees 40 to 45 minutes or until firm. Cool. Cut tops from cream puffs; spoon Mandarin Filling (see opposite) into bottoms. Replace tops. Serve immediately.

Serves 8.

Melt butter in large skillet. Add almonds; cook and stir until golden brown. Stir in remaining ingredients, except oranges. Heat to serving temperature. Gently stir in oranges.

Smoked Turkey Sukiyaki

    3 tbsp vegetable oil
    1 cup green pepper, minced
    1 cup celery, sliced
    1 can (4 oz) mushrooms, sliced
    1 cup green onions, chopped in 1-inch
        pieces
    1½ cups smoked turkey
    1/4 cup soy sauce
    2½ cups hot rice

Heat oil in skillet; add vegetables and cook over medium heat 6 to 8 minutes or until crisp-tender. Stir in turkey and soy sauce. Heat through and serve at once over hot rice.

Serves 4.

Chinese Smoked Chicken

1 cup water
1 envelope (1½ oz) spaghetti sauce mix
1 cup half and half cream
2 tbsp butter or margarine
1 tsp soy sauce
2 cups smoked chicken, chopped
1 pkg (9 oz) frozen Italian green beans, thawed
1 can (3 oz) chow mein noodles, heated

Combine water, spaghetti sauce mix, cream, butter, and soy sauce in large skillet. Heat to boiling, stirring constantly. Reduce heat and simmer 5 minutes. Add chicken and beans; cook 5 minutes longer or until beans are tender. Serve on bed of oven-heated chow mein noodles.

Serves 4 to 6.

American Smoked Chicken Chop Suey

1 pkg (4 oz) noodles
2½ cups tomatoes, canned
1/4 lb cheese, grated
1/4 cup cooking oil
1/2 cup onion, diced
1/2 cup celery, diced
1/4 cup green pepper, diced
1½ cups smoked chicken, cubed
1 tbsp soy sauce
1/2 tsp chili powder
1 tbsp salt
1 tsp sugar
1/4 tsp pepper

Cook noodles in boiling salted water until tender. Drain, rinse and drain again; return to saucepan. Add tomatoes and grated cheese; stir over low heat until cheese is melted. Heat oil in skillet; add onion, celery, and green pepper. Simmer over low heat until soft and lightly browned, about 10 minutes. Add smoked chicken and seasonings; combine with noodle mixture.

Serves 6 to 8.

Smoked Chicken Chow Mein

1/4 cup butter

1 medium onion, chopped

2 cups celery, diced

Basic Seasoning or salt and pepper to
taste

1½ cups hot water

1 can (1 lb) bean sprouts, drained

2 cups smoked chicken, cubed

2 tsp cold water

2 tbsp cornstarch

1 tbsp soy sauce

1 tsp sugar

Chow mein noodles

Melt butter in skillet; add onion and cook 3 minutes. Add celery, seasoning, and hot water; cover and cook 5 minutes. Add bean sprouts and smoked chicken; mix thoroughly and cook 5 minutes. Combine cold water, cornstarch, soy sauce, and sugar; add to smoked chicken mixture. Stir lightly and cook 1 minute. Serve hot over chow mein noodles.

Serves 4 to 6.

Lobster and Smoked Chicken Cantonese

1 clove garlic, minced

1/4 cup butter

1 can (5 oz) water chestnuts, drained,
sliced

1 can (5 oz) bamboo shoots, drained

1/4 lb mushrooms, sliced

1 pkg frozen peas, slightly thawed

3 cups chicken broth

Salt to taste

1/4 cup cold water

1/4 cup cornstarch

1 tbsp soy sauce

1 can (6½ oz) lobster meat, drained

1 smoked chicken breast, sliced

1 can (5 oz) chow mein noodles

2 hard-cooked eggs, chopped

In skillet sauté garlic in butter for 1 minute. Add water chestnuts, bamboo sprouts, mushrooms, and peas. Cook for 3 minutes. Add broth and salt; cook for 1 minute. Combine water, cornstarch, and soy sauce; add to vegetable mixture. Cook over medium heat until thickened, stirring constantly. Fold in lobster and smoked chicken. Cook until heated through. Serve over chow mein noodles and garnish with eggs.

Serves 6.

Chinese Duck with Almonds

1/2 cup mushrooms, sliced
1/2 cup onion, minced
1/2 cup celery, sliced
1/2 cup canned water chestnuts, drained, diced
1 cup bean sprouts, drained
6 tbsp oil, divided
1/2 cup plus 2 tbsp cold water, divided
1 cup smoked duck, diced
1 can (10½ oz) consommé or 1¼ cups chicken broth
1/2 cup almonds, blanched
1 tsp cornstarch
Salt to taste
1/4 tsp sugar
1/2 cup soy sauce
2 cups steamed rice or fried noodles

Lightly brown mushrooms, onion, celery, water chestnuts, and bean sprouts in 2 tbsp oil. Add 1/2 cup water, cover, and simmer 10 minutes. Brown duck lightly in 2 tbsp oil. Add consommé, cover, and let simmer 10 minutes. Brown almonds slightly in remaining oil and set aside. Mix cornstarch, salt, sugar, 2 tbsp water, and soy sauce; add to duck and cook, stirring until slightly thickened and smooth. Add drained vegetables; heat thoroughly; add almonds and serve with steamed rice or fried noodles.

Serves 4 to 6.

Smoked Turkey Chow Mein

1/4 cup butter
2½ cups smoked turkey, cut in thin strips
1 cup onion, chopped
3 cups celery, diced
Basic Seasoning or salt and pepper to taste
1¾ cups hot water or chicken broth
1 can (1 lb) mixed Chinese vegetables, drained
2 tbsp cold water
2 tbsp cornstarch
2 tsp soy sauce
1 tsp sugar
Chow mein noodles

Melt butter in skillet; add smoked turkey and onion; cook 5 minutes. Add celery, seasoning, and hot water; cover and cook for 10 minutes. Add Chinese mixed vegetables; mix thoroughly and heat to boiling. Combine cold water, cornstarch, soy sauce, and sugar; add to smoked turkey mixture. Stir lightly and cook 2 minutes. Serve hot over chow mein noodles.

Serves 6.

Creamed Dishes

Smoked Turkey or Chicken à la King

1/2 cup mushrooms, sliced
4 tbsp fat or cooking oil
3 tbsp flour
Salt to taste
2 tsp Worcestershire sauce
2 cups milk, scalded
1/2 cup green pepper, chopped
1/2 cup stuffed olives, chopped
2 cups smoked turkey or chicken, diced
4 to 6 slices hot buttered toast

Sauté mushrooms in fat for 5 minutes. Blend in flour, salt, and Worcestershire sauce. Add milk and cook until thickened, stirring constantly. Add green pepper, olives, and turkey. Cook until heated through. Serve on toast.

Serves 4 to 6.

Smoked Turkey or Chicken à la King with Cheese and Pimiento

1/4 cup green pepper, diced
2 tbsp butter
3 cans (10½ oz each) cheddar cheese soup
3/4 to 1 cup milk
3 cups smoked turkey or chicken, diced
1/4 cup pimiento, chopped
1/8 tsp pepper
Hot biscuits or toast

In large saucepan sauté green pepper in butter until tender. Blend in soup and milk; stir until smooth. Add smoked turkey, pimiento, and pepper. Heat slowly, stirring occasionally. Serve on toast or hot biscuits.

Serves 10.

Minced Smoked Chicken and Mushrooms

1 tbsp butter
1 tbsp flour
Basic Seasoning or salt and pepper to taste
1 can (6 oz) mushrooms, sliced
1 cup milk, scalded
2 cups smoked chicken, diced

Melt butter in skillet; add flour and seasoning. Add mushroom liquid and milk; cook until thickened, stirring constantly. Heat to boiling and add mushrooms and smoked chicken; cook 3 minutes. Serve hot on toast points.

Serves 6.

Smoked Chicken à la King with Onions

2 tbsp shortening
1/4 cup onions, chopped
1/2 cup green pepper, chopped
1/2 cup celery, chopped
1 tbsp butter
1 tbsp flour
2 cups milk, scalded
Basic Seasoning or salt and pepper to taste
2 egg yolks, beaten
2 tbsp pimiento, chopped
1/4 cup mushrooms
2 cups smoked chicken, diced
2 tbsp parsley, chopped

Set heat selector of electric fry pan at 225 degrees. Melt shortening and sauté onions, green pepper, and celery until tender. Remove and set aside. Melt butter in fry pan; blend in flour and add milk slowly, stirring constantly, until thickened. Add seasoning. Mix a small quantity of hot milk mixture with egg yolks, then combine with sauce, stirring constantly. Add sautéed vegetables, pimiento, mushrooms, smoked chicken, and parsley. Serve on toast or hot biscuits. Garnish with toasted slivered almonds.

Serves 4 to 6.

Smoked Turkey or Chicken, Hungarian Style

1/4 cup butter or margarine
1/2 cup onion, diced
1 can (6 oz) mushrooms, sliced
1/4 cup flour
2 tsp paprika
Salt to taste
1 tsp sugar
1½ cups milk, scalded
1 cup sour cream
2½ cups smoked turkey or chicken, diced
4 cups hot buttered noodles

Melt butter in heavy saucepan. Add onion and mushroom slices; cook and stir until onion is transparent. Blend in flour, paprika, salt, and sugar. Add milk. Cook, stirring constantly, until smooth and thickened. Slowly stir in sour cream. Continue to stir until sauce is smooth. Add smoked turkey and heat to serving temperature. Serve on hot buttered noodles.

Serves 6.

Especially Good Creamed Chicken

1/4 cup green pepper, minced
1 tbsp butter or margarine
1 can (10½ oz) cream of chicken soup
1/4 cup milk
1 cup smoked chicken, diced
1/4 cup pimiento, chopped
6 patty shells or toast

Cook green pepper until tender in butter in a saucepan. Stir in soup, then milk. Heat slowly, stirring constantly. Add chicken and pimiento; continue cooking about 10 minutes. Pour creamed chicken into patty shells. Serve garnished with sprigs of parsley, if desired.

Serves 6.

Creamed Smoked Chicken

1/2 cup celery, chopped
1 tsp onion, chopped
1 tbsp green pepper, chopped
2 tbsp fat
1/4 cup flour
1½ cups chicken broth, heated
1/2 cup milk or cream, heated
1½ cups smoked chicken, diced
Basic Seasoning or salt and pepper to taste
Rice, toast, or biscuits

Sauté celery, onion, and green pepper in fat until tender. Blend in flour. Stir in the heated chicken broth and milk or cream and cook to a smooth sauce, stirring constantly. Add smoked chicken to sauce and season to taste. Heat the mixture thoroughly and serve on rice, toast, or biscuits.

Serves 4.

Smoked Chicken à la King with Mushrooms

1 can (2 oz) mushrooms, drained
1/4 cup green pepper, chopped
1/4 cup butter
1/4 cup flour
Basic Seasoning or salt and pepper to taste
1 cup chicken broth, heated
1 cup cream or canned milk, heated
1 cup smoked chicken, diced
1/4 cup pimiento, chopped

Sauté mushrooms and green pepper in butter; blend in flour and seasoning. Slowly stir in heated chicken broth and cream; bring to boil over low heat, stirring constantly. Boil 1 minute. Add smoked chicken and pimiento; heat through. Serve in toast cups or patty shells.

Serves 6.

Smoked Pheasant à la King

1 green pepper, minced.
1 cup mushrooms, sliced
2 tbsp butter or margarine
2 tbsp flour
1 cup chicken stock or bouillon, heated
2 cups smoked pheasant, diced
1 cup evaporated milk or sour cream
2 egg yolks
4 tbsp dry sherry
1 pimiento, diced
Basic Seasoning or salt and pepper to taste

In skillet sauté green pepper and mushrooms in melted butter until tender. Remove and set aside. Add flour to butter in skillet; add stock and cook, stirring until smooth and thickened. Add smoked pheasant and cooked vegetables; heat thoroughly. Remove from heat; add cream mixed with beaten egg yolks and remaining ingredients. Serve at once or keep hot in top of double boiler. (Do not boil after adding egg yolks.) Serve on toast or hot biscuits.

Serves 4 to 6.

Pastry Dishes

Smoked Turkey Crepes

Crepes

4 tbsp butter
3 eggs
1 cup milk
1 cup flour
1/4 tsp salt

Melt butter in 8-inch skillet or crepe pan. Beat eggs until light; add milk and melted butter, then flour and salt. Beat until batter is smooth. Spoon batter onto hot greased skillet and tip so that a thin coating of batter covers bottom of pan; cook 1 minute or until brown. Remove from pan and place upside down on clean towel; continue until all crepes are made.

Filling

6 tbsp butter or margarine, divided
1/4 cup flour
1/2 cup turkey or chicken stock, heated
1 can (10½ oz) cream of chicken soup
1/2 cup sour cream
2 cups smoked turkey, diced
1 tsp lemon juice
1/4 cup almonds, toasted

Melt 4 tbsp butter in medium saucepan; blend in flour. Add turkey stock and cook, stirring until thickened. Turn heat down and cook for 1 minute. Remove from heat and stir in soup, sour cream, turkey, lemon juice, and nuts. Mixture should be thick and cooled. Spoon turkey mixture across center of browned side of each crepe and roll up; continue until all crepes are filled. In a large skillet melt 2 tbsp butter, adding more as needed; brown crepes on all sides until golden brown. Transfer to chafing dish to keep hot.

Serves 10.

Smoked Turkey Pie

1/4 cup onion, chopped
2 tbsp butter
3 eggs
1 envelope (7/8 oz) poultry gravy mix
1 cup milk
2 cups smoked turkey, cubed
1 unbaked 9-inch pie shell
1/4 cup cheddar or Swiss cheese, shredded

Cook onion in butter until tender. Beat together eggs, gravy mix, and milk. Stir in turkey and onions. Pour into pie shell and sprinkle with cheese. Bake at 375 degrees for 25 to 35 minutes or until knife inserted in center comes out clean.

Serves 4 to 6.

Herb Crust Smoked Turkey Pie

Herb Crust

2¼ cups flour
1 envelope onion salad dressing mix
3/4 cup shortening, divided
7 tbsp cold water

Combine flour and salad dressing mix. Cut in 1/2 cup shortening, using light strokes of pastry blender until mixture resembles coarse meal. Add remaining shortening in several pieces and cut in lightly until divided into pieces the size of peas. Sprinkle in water, a small amount at a time, mixing lightly until particles cling together when pastry is pressed into a ball. Cover with a damp cloth and let stand a few minutes before using. Roll out half the pastry and place in a 10-inch pie pan or a shallow 1½-qt casserole. Roll remainder to cover filling. Fill bottom crust with Smoked Turkey Filling (see below). Top with remaining pastry. Trim, flute, and seal edges. Roll out scraps and cut into designs to decorate top of pastry, if desired. Bake at 450 degrees for 10 minutes; reduce temperature to 350 degrees and continue baking 15 minutes longer or until crust is golden brown.

Smoked Turkey Filling

1 chicken bouillon cube
1 cup hot water
3 tbsp butter
3 tbsp flour
Salt to taste
1 cup milk, heated
2 cups smoked turkey
1 can (4 oz) mushrooms, drained, sliced
2 tbsp dry sherry
1 tbsp pimiento, chopped

Dissolve bouillon cube in hot water. In skillet melt butter; stir in flour and salt. Cook and stir over low heat until blended. Stir in bouillon and milk. Cook, stirring constantly, until thickened and smooth. Add turkey, mushrooms, sherry, and pimiento. Cool.

Serves 6 to 8.

Smoked Pigeon Pot Pie

2 smoked pigeons
2 carrots, diced
1 large onion, diced
1 potato, diced
2 cups flour
1/4 tsp salt
2½ tsp baking powder
2 tbsp shortening
1 cup milk

Remove bones from smoked pigeons and cut meat into pieces. Put carrots, onion, and potato in kettle; cook until tender in a minimum amount of water. While the vegetables are cooking, prepare biscuit topping by combining flour, salt, and baking powder. Cut in shortening; add milk. Roll out dough and cut into biscuits. When vegetables are cooked, combine with smoked pigeon meat and place in a 3-inch-deep baking dish, using most of liquid. Top with biscuits and bake in 375-degree oven until biscuits are done, about 20 minutes. The vegetable-meat mixture should be hot before placing biscuits on top.

Serves 3 to 4.

Smoked Chicken Rolls

1 cup smoked chicken, diced
3 tbsp butter, divided
2 tbsp water
Basic Seasoning or salt and pepper to taste
1 cup milk
1 egg
1 cup pancake mix
1 cup whole cranberry sauce

In saucepan heat together chicken, 2 tbsp butter, and water; add seasoning to taste. For pancake rolls, combine milk, egg, pancake mix, and 1 tbsp melted butter, stirring until fairly smooth. Bake 8 pancakes, using 1/4 cup batter for each. Place 1 heaping tbsp chicken mixture on each pancake; roll up. Top with warm cranberry sauce.

Serves 4.

Smoked Chicken Shortcakes

1 can (8 oz) oven-ready biscuits
1 can (10½ oz) cream of chicken soup
1/2 cup evaporated milk
1 cup smoked chicken, diced
1 can (8 oz) peas, drained
Basic Seasoning or salt and pepper to taste

Bake biscuits as package directs. Meanwhile, combine soup, milk, smoked chicken, and peas in a saucepan, heating until bubbly; season to taste. Break open hot biscuits and generously spoon hot chicken mixture over hot biscuit halves.

Serves 5.

Smoked Pheasant Meringue Pie

1/4 cup butter
1 large onion, sliced
1/4 cup flour
2 cups chicken bouillon, heated
1/2 tsp basil leaves
1/4 tsp pepper
3 eggs, separated
1/3 cup pimiento-stuffed olives, sliced
3 cups smoked pheasant in 1-inch cubes
3 tbsp parsley, chopped
1 unbaked 9-inch pie shell
1/4 cup Parmesan cheese, grated
1/4 cup blanched almonds, slivered
Pimiento-stuffed olives for garnish

To prepare filling for pie, melt butter in large saucepan. Add onion and sauté until golden brown. Blend in flour. Gradually stir in bouillon and seasonings; simmer sauce 1 minute. Beat egg yolks in large bowl and gradually stir in 1/3 hot sauce, then mix with remaining sauce in pan. Add 1/3 cup sliced olives, smoked pheasant, and parsley; mix thoroughly. Spoon into pie shell. Bake at 425 degrees 35 minutes. Beat egg whites until stiff peaks form; fold in cheese. (*Note:* Meringue will lose volume and stiffness when cheese is added.) Spread mixture over surface of pie. Sprinkle almonds on top; place olives in border around edge of pie. Bake about 5 minutes more or until topping is lightly browned. Remove pie from oven. Allow pie to stand for 15 minutes before cutting.

Serves 6.

Smoked Turkey and Savory Biscuits

1 tbsp onion, grated
1/4 cup butter or margarine
1/4 cup flour
1/4 tsp white pepper
1/4 tsp dry mustard
1/8 tsp nutmeg
2 cans (10½ oz) chicken gravy, heated
1 can (4 oz) mushrooms, sliced
1/4 cup dry sherry
1/3 cup stuffed olives, sliced
2 cups smoked turkey, cubed
Savory Biscuits (see below)

In skillet sauté onion in butter 5 minutes until transparent. Combine flour, pepper, mustard, and nutmeg; blend into butter mixture. Stir in chicken gravy, blending thoroughly over low heat. Add mushrooms with liquid, sherry, olives, and turkey. Heat and serve over hot, split Savory Biscuits.

Serves 4 to 6.

Savory Biscuits

Add 1 tsp poultry seasoning for each cup of biscuit mix used. Prepare according to package directions. Roll out 1/2-inch thick. Cut with 3-inch biscuit cutter. Bake as directed.

Smoked Turkey Pasty

1/4 cup Parmesan cheese, grated
1 pkg piecrust mix
4 tbsp butter or margarine, divided
1/2 cup onions, minced
1/2 cup celery, chopped
1/2 cup pecans, chopped
3 cups smoked turkey, chopped
1½ tsp caraway seeds
Basic Seasoning or salt and pepper to taste
1/4 lb mushrooms, fresh
1 cup cheese sauce, heated
1/4 cup pimiento, sliced

Add cheese to piecrust mix. Make pastry as package directs. Form into ball; wrap in waxed paper and refrigerate. Preheat oven to 425 degrees. Meanwhile, in skillet heat 2 tbsp butter and sauté onions, celery, and pecans until golden. Add turkey, caraway seeds, and seasoning. Cool slightly. On floured surface, roll pastry to make a 13-inch square. Transfer to large greased baking sheet. Place turkey filling on pastry, covering half, from corner to corner. Turn opposite corner over to cover, making a triangle. Seal edges, using tines of fork. Bake 25 to 30 minutes, or until browned. Meanwhile, in 2 tbsp butter, sauté whole mushrooms until tender. To hot cheese sauce, add pimiento. Serve pasty garnished with cheese sauce and mushrooms.

Serves 8.

Smoked Chicken Pie with Sweet Potato Crust

3 cups smoked chicken, diced
1 cup carrots, cooked, diced
6 small white onions, cooked
1 tbsp parsley, chopped
1 cup evaporated milk
1 cup chicken stock
2 tbsp flour
Basic Seasoning or salt and pepper to taste
Sweet Potato Crust (see below)

Arrange chicken, carrots, onions, and parsley in layers in casserole. Combine milk and chicken stock; add slowly to flour, blending well. Cook until thickened, stirring constantly. Season and pour over chicken and vegetables in casserole. Cover with Sweet Potato Crust. Bake in 350-degree oven about 40 minutes.

Serves 6 to 8.

Sweet Potato Crust

1 cup flour, sifted
1 tsp baking powder
1/2 tsp salt
1 cup cold sweet potato, mashed
1/3 cup melted fat
1 egg, well beaten

Sift flour with baking powder and salt. Work in mashed sweet potato, fat, and egg. Roll 1/4-inch thick and cover chicken pie.

Croquettes

Smoked Chicken Croquettes

1/2 cup mushrooms, minced
2 cups smoked chicken, minced
1 tbsp parsley, chopped
1 cup milk
Basic Seasoning or salt and pepper to taste
4 tbsp butter or margarine
1½ tbsp flour
1 whole egg and 2 egg yolks
1¼ cups olive oil
Bread crumbs

Combine mushrooms, chicken, and parsley in mixing bowl. Soak the mixture with milk and season to taste. Melt butter in skillet and blend in flour. Remove from heat and blend in chicken mixture. Cook 2 or 3 minutes until thickened and smooth, stirring constantly. Remove from heat. Cool until lukewarm; then add 2 egg yolks, blending well. Chill thoroughly. Form into croquettes, rolling them in the hands. Beat together 1 egg and olive oil in a deep dish with seasoning. Flour croquettes lightly. Dip in the egg-oil mixture and roll in bread crumbs, taking care not to coat them too thickly. Fry in deep oil heated to 370 degrees until golden brown. Drain on absorbent paper.

Serves 4.

Chicken or Turkey Croquettes

2 tbsp cooking oil
2 tsp onion, minced
4 tbsp flour
Basic Seasoning or salt and pepper to taste
1 cup milk, scalded
2 cups smoked chicken or turkey, minced
1 tsp parsley, minced
Bread crumbs, finely ground
1 egg
2 tbsp milk or water
Oil for deep-fat frying
Parsley sprigs

In skillet heat 2 tbsp oil; add minced onion and sauté until lightly browned. Blend in flour and seasoning. Gradually add milk and cook, stirring constantly, until mixture thickens. Add smoked chicken or turkey and parsley. Chill thoroughly. Form into croquettes. Roll in crumbs, then beaten egg combined with water, and again in crumbs. Fry in deep oil heated to 370 degrees until golden brown. Drain on absorbent paper. Arrange on hot platter; garnish with parsley.

Makes 6 to 8.

Hash

Smoked Duck Hash

2 cups potatoes, cooked, diced
2 cups smoked duck, diced
1/4 cup melted butter
3/4 cup milk
2 tbsp onion, grated
1/4 cup green pepper, chopped
Basic Seasoning or salt and pepper to
 taste

Combine all ingredients and place in a greased 1½-qt casserole. Bake at 375 degrees for 20 minutes or until bubbling hot.

Serves 4.

Smoked Chicken Hash

1½ cups smoked chicken, chopped
1 cup boiled potatoes, diced
2 tbsp fat
1 tbsp parsley, minced
Basic Seasoning or salt and pepper to
 taste
1/2 cup stock or water

Mix chicken and potatoes together. Melt fat, add chicken mixture, parsley, seasoning, and stock. Cook until browned. (Add 1/4 cup chopped green pepper, if desired.)

Serves 4.

Baked Smoked Chicken Hash

2 cups smoked chicken, chopped
1 medium onion, chopped
1 raw potato, chopped
2 pimientos, diced
2 carrots, shredded
Basic Seasoning or salt and pepper to
 taste
2 tbsp parsley, chopped
1/2 tsp poultry seasoning
1 can chicken gravy or 1 cup leftover
 chicken gravy, heated

Combine all ingredients and mix well. Put in 1½-qt casserole; cover and bake in 350-degree oven 45 minutes. Uncover and bake 15 minutes longer.

Serves 4 to 6.

Smoked Turkey Hash

3 cups smoked turkey, diced
1/2 cup soft bread crumbs
1/2 cup green pepper, chopped
1/2 cup onion, chopped
2 tbsp parsley, chopped
1/2 tsp sage
Basic Seasoning or salt and pepper to
 taste
4 tbsp butter, divided
2 tbsp flour
1½ cups cream or milk, scalded

Toss the smoked turkey, crumbs, green pepper, onion, parsley, and seasonings into a large bowl. In saucepan melt 2 tbsp butter. Blend in flour; add cream and stir until thickened. Add to turkey mixture and stir. Melt remaining 2 tbsp butter in large frying pan. When it is bubbling, toss in the turkey mixture and cook, uncovered, for 25 minutes.

Serves 4 to 5.

Smoked Chicken Hashed in Cream

2 cups smoked chicken, diced
1 cup light cream
3 tbsp butter or margarine
3 tbsp flour
Basic Seasoning or salt and pepper to
 taste
1½ cups milk, heated
3 egg yolks, beaten, divided
1 tsp instant minced onion
2 tbsp Parmesan cheese, grated, divided

Simmer the smoked chicken in cream until the cream is reduced to about one-half the original volume. Melt butter and blend in flour and seasoning. Gradually add milk and cook, stirring until thickened. Add about 1/2 cup of this sauce to the chicken mixture and stir in 1 egg yolk and onion. Beat a little of the sauce into remaining 2 egg yolks. Put back in saucepan with remaining sauce and cook a few minutes longer. Stir in 1 tbsp cheese. Pour chicken mixture into shallow baking dish, cover with sauce; top with remaining 1 tbsp cheese. Brown under broiler.

Serves 4.

Curried and Rice Dishes

Smoked Duck Curry with Sour Cream

1/4 cup onion, chopped
3 tbsp butter or margarine
2 tsp curry powder
3 tbsp flour
1½ cups chicken broth or bouillon, heated
Salt to taste
3 cups smoked duck, diced
1 cup sour cream
Parsley or chives, chopped
2 cups cooked rice

In skillet sauté onion in butter with curry powder until transparent. Stir in flour; cook 2 minutes, stirring. Blend in broth and salt. Cook and stir until sauce thickens. Add duck; heat through. Blend in sour cream, gently heating. Sprinkle with chopped parsley or chives. Serve with buttered rice.

Serves 5 to 6.

Smoked Chicken Curry in a Hurry

2 cups smoked chicken, cubed
1 can (10½ oz) cream of chicken soup
1 tsp curry powder
1/4 cup dry white wine
3 cups steamed rice

Combine smoked chicken, soup, curry powder, and wine. Gently heat over low heat until hot. Serve over steamed rice with a choice of condiments such as coconut, orange sections, chutney, chopped salted peanuts, and cooked crumbled bacon.

Serves 6 to 8.

Smoked Chicken Pilaf

2 cups smoked chicken, cut in strips
1/2 cup butter
1/2 cup walnuts, chopped
1 tbsp instant minced onion
Basic Seasoning or salt and pepper to taste
1/4 tsp ground coriander
2 cups rice, uncooked
4 cups chicken bouillon, boiling
2 medium tomatoes, peeled, seeded, chopped

Cook chicken in butter over low heat 3 minutes. Add walnuts and cook 2 minutes longer. Add onion, seasoning, and coriander; add rice and cook 5 minutes, stirring. Pour in boiling bouillon. Add tomatoes; bring to boil, cover, and simmer 20 minutes, or until rice is tender and liquid completely absorbed. Remove from heat and let stand 5 minutes before serving.

Serves 4 to 6.

Curried Smoked Turkey

4 tbsp butter
4 tbsp flour
1 tsp curry powder
Salt to taste
1/8 tsp paprika
Pinch cayenne pepper
1 cup turkey stock, heated
1 cup milk, heated
1/4 cup ripe olives, sliced
1/4 cup pimiento, chopped
1/4 cup button mushrooms
1¼ cups smoked turkey, chopped
2 cups cooked rice
1/4 cup dry sherry (optional)

In saucepan mix together melted butter, flour, and seasonings to form a soft paste. Add stock to paste in saucepan over medium heat, stirring until smooth; add milk, stirring constantly. Cook gently until sauce is thickened. Add olives, pimiento, mushrooms, and turkey. Serve over mounds of cooked rice. Sherry may be added to turkey mixture just before serving.

Serves 4 to 6.

Smoked Chicken with Rice

Chicken bones from smoked chicken
Water
Basic Seasoning or salt and pepper to taste
1 onion, minced
1½ tbsp melted chicken fat or oil
1/2 cup rice, uncooked
1½ cups smoked chicken, diced
Grated cheddar cheese

Cover bones with water and simmer 1 hour or longer, adding water if necessary to make 1 quart of broth; strain. Add seasoning to taste. In large frying pan cook onion in fat or oil a few minutes; add chicken broth and bring to rapid boil. Slowly sprinkle in the rice. Cover and simmer about 25 minutes or until grains swell and become soft. Stir with a fork from time to time to keep the rice from sticking. When rice is done, it will have absorbed the broth and the grains will be large and flaky. Then add the smoked chicken and more seasoning, if needed. Turn mixture onto a hot platter; sprinkle generously with grated cheese.

Serves 4 to 6.

To clean a grater after grating cheese, rub it with a piece of dry toast or a raw potato.

Golden Glow Turkey

1⅔ cups sliced carrots
1/4 cup butter
1/4 cup onion, chopped
1 cup orange juice
1 cup water
2 tsp sugar
1 tsp salt
1 tsp orange rind, grated
1/2 tsp poultry seasoning
1/8 tsp pepper
1½ cups smoked turkey, diced
1⅓ cups cooked rice

Sauté carrots in butter in large skillet over medium heat about 5 minutes or until almost tender, turning frequently. Add onion and sauté until lightly browned. Add orange juice, water, sugar, salt, orange rind, seasoning, and pepper; bring to a boil. Stir in smoked turkey and rice. Cover and simmer 8 minutes or until rice and carrots are tender.

Serves 4.

Hawaiian Smoked Turkey

1/4 cup butter
1/4 cup flour
2 cups turkey stock, heated
Basic Seasoning or salt and pepper to taste
1/8 tsp nutmeg
1 cup crushed pineapple, drained
2 cups smoked turkey, diced
1/2 cup toasted coconut
2 cups hot rice

In skillet melt butter; add flour and stir until well blended. Gradually add stock; cook, stirring constantly, until thickened and smooth. Season to taste. Heat pineapple and turkey in sauce. Sprinkle with toasted coconut. Serve on hot rice.

Serves 4 to 5.

Smoked Chicken Curry

1/4 cup onion, chopped
1 medium apple, diced
3 tbsp butter or margarine
3 tbsp flour
1 to 2 tbsp curry powder
2 cups chicken broth or bouillon, heated
1/2 cup pine nuts or almonds, blanched, slivered
1 cup cream
2 cups smoked chicken, slivered
3 cups cooked rice

In skillet sauté onion and apple in butter 5 minutes. Sprinkle in flour and curry powder, stirring until blended. Add chicken broth and pine nuts, stirring until thickened over medium heat. Slowly add the cream; stir until thickened. Add smoked chicken to sauce; heat. Serve over hot cooked rice.

Serves 6 to 8.

Smoked Turkey in Curry

3/4 cup onion, chopped
1/2 cup celery, chopped
1/4 cup butter or margarine
6 tbsp flour
2 cups turkey broth or chicken bouillon,
   heated
2 tsp curry powder
1/4 tsp ginger
2 cups smoked turkey, slivered
Basic Seasoning or salt and pepper to
   taste
1/2 cup green grapes, halved, seeded
3 cups cooked rice

Sauté onion and celery in butter in heavy 2-qt saucepan over low heat until transparent. Remove from heat. Stir in flour; then blend broth into mixture. Add curry powder and ginger. Return to heat; cook, stirring constantly, until mixture boils and thickens. Add turkey and seasoning; simmer 10 minutes. Add grapes; heat through. Serve over hot cooked rice.

Serves 6.

Dishes Prepared with Wine

Smoked Turkey Supreme on Corn Bread

3 cups turkey gravy
1 cup celery, diced
2 tsp instant minced onion
1 bay leaf
1 tsp paprika
1/2 cup dry white wine
Basic Seasoning or salt and pepper to
   taste
3 cups smoked turkey, diced
1 cup ham, diced
1/2 cup ripe olives, sliced
Hot corn bread squares

Combine gravy, celery, onion, bay leaf, and paprika; simmer 15 minutes. Remove bay leaf. Add wine; stir to blend. Season to taste. Stir in turkey, ham, and ripe olives. Heat mixture thoroughly. Serve on squares of hot corn bread.

Serves 6.

When smoking a turkey, reserve the neck and giblets. Cook them in a generous amount of water until tender; season with Basic Seasoning. If additional water is desired, potato liquid may be added. Use diced giblets and stock in a favorite turkey gravy recipe mixed with small amount of cheddar cheese soup. Serve over toast or biscuits. Make plenty;' it may be used with chicken, goose, duck, or any smoked poultry.

Smoked Pheasant Delight

1/4 cup butter
2 tbsp green onion, chopped
1/4 cup flour
2 tsp chicken stock base or chicken
   bouillon
Salt to taste
1/4 tsp marjoram
Dash garlic powder
1¾ cups boiling water
1/4 cup dry white wine
6 to 8 large smoked pheasant slices
1/4 cup slivered almonds, toasted

In a large skillet melt butter; sauté onion. Blend in flour, chicken stock base, salt, marjoram, and garlic powder; cook over low heat until mixture is smooth. Add water, stirring constantly; boil and stir 1 minute. Decrease heat; add wine. Place pheasant in sauce; cover and heat 10 to 15 minutes until pheasant is heated through. Remove to serving platter; sprinkle with almonds. .

Serves 6 to 8.

Smoked Chicken Livers Sautéed

4 tbsp butter or margarine
1 lb smoked chicken livers
3 tbsp flour
1 cup consommé or bouillon cube broth,
   heated
1/2 cup dry sherry
1 can (3 oz) mushrooms, sliced, drained
2 tbsp parsley, chopped
Basic Seasoning or salt and pepper to taste
Toast or rice

Heat butter in skillet; add livers and sauté quickly, turning frequently. Remove from pan. Add flour to drippings, blending well. Add consommé and sherry; cook, stirring constantly, until mixture is thickened and smooth. Add livers, mushrooms, parsley, and seasoning to sauce; heat piping hot. Serve on toast or with rice.

Serves 6.

Smoked Duck with Red Wine

1 medium onion, chopped
2 tbsp butter or margarine
2 tbsp flour
2 cups chicken consommé, heated
Juice and rind of 1 medium orange, diced
1/4 cup red table wine
2 medium-size smoked ducks, disjointed
Basic Seasoning or salt and pepper to taste
Rice

Sauté onion in butter; add flour and stir until brown. Add consommé and simmer 10 minutes. Add orange juice, orange rind, wine, and duck to sauce. Season to taste and simmer gently 30 minutes. Serve with rice.

Serves 4 to 6.

Salads

Molded Smoked Turkey Salad

2 envelopes unflavored gelatin
1½ cups cold water
2 tbsp lemon juice
1 tsp sugar
Salt to taste
1/2 tsp dry mustard
1/2 tsp paprika
1/4 tsp onion salt
1 tsp horseradish
4 or 5 drops tabasco sauce
2 cups sour cream
2 cups smoked turkey, diced
1/3 cup celery, diced
1/2 cup cucumber, unpeeled, diced
2 pimientos, chopped
2 tbsp green pepper, chopped
Lettuce cups
Tomato wedges
4 hard-cooked eggs, chopped

Soften gelatin in water and dissolve over hot water. Add lemon juice, sugar, salt, mustard, paprika, onion salt, horseradish, tabasco sauce, and sour cream; mix well. Chill until mixture begins to set; fold in remaining ingredients, except lettuce, tomatoes, and eggs. Pour into 8 individual molds and chill until firm. Unmold into lettuce cups and garnish with tomato wedges and chopped egg.

Serves 8.

German Chicken Salad

1/2 lb mushrooms, sliced
1 to 2 tbsp butter
4 cups smoked chicken, diced
1½ cups celery, chopped
1 cup mayonnaise
1 cup whipping cream, whipped to make
  2 cups
Lettuce
Capers

Sauté mushrooms in butter for 2 to 3 minutes; cool. Mix the mushrooms, chicken, and celery with mayonnaise. Chill several hours in refrigerator. Fold in the whipped cream just before serving. Serve on bed of lettuce and garnish with capers.

Serves 6 to 8.

Chilled Smoked Chicken and Fruit Salad

3 cups smoked chicken, chopped
1 apple, diced
1/4 cup toasted almonds, sliced
1 large orange, peeled, sectioned
15 large grapes, halved, seeded
1 banana, sliced
1 cup mayonnaise
8 lettuce cups

Combine all ingredients except lettuce and lightly toss. Serve chilled on lettuce.

Serves 8.

California Smoked Chicken Salad

3 tbsp lemon juice
1 cup smoked chicken, diced
1/2 cup apple, diced
1/2 cup ripe olives, chopped
1/2 cup celery, chopped
2 tbsp mayonnaise, thinned with 2 tbsp
   cream

Sprinkle lemon juice over chicken and apple, mixing lightly. Combine with remaining ingredients, using mayonnaise to moisten; toss lightly. Serve cold dolloped with additional mayonnaise.

Serves 4.

Curried Smoked Chicken Salad

1/2 cup onion, minced
1¼ tsp curry powder
2 tbsp butter
1/3 cup mayonnaise
1 tbsp lemon juice
Dash ground cayenne pepper
3 cups smoked chicken, diced
1 can (13¼ oz) pineapple chunks
1/2 cup peanuts, chopped
1/3 cup seedless white raisins
1 red apple, cored, diced
Lettuce leaves
2 tbsp shredded coconut

Mix onion with curry powder and sauté in butter 3 to 5 minutes; cool. Combine curry mixture with mayonnaise, lemon juice, and pepper; mix well and set aside. In large salad bowl combine chicken, pineapple, peanuts, raisins, and apple. Add dressing; mix and toss gently. Serve in lettuce-lined bowl and garnish with coconut.

Serves 8.

Smoked Turkey Cranberry Mold

2 envelopes unflavored gelatin
1 cup water, divided
1 cup mayonnaise
1/2 cup milk
2 tbsp lemon juice
Salt to taste
1 cup smoked turkey, chopped
1/2 cup celery, chopped
1/2 cup apple, chopped
1 tbsp onion, chopped
1 can (1 lb) jellied cranberry sauce

Soften 1 envelope of gelatin in 1/2 cup water. Stir over low heat until dissolved. Mix together mayonnaise, milk, lemon juice, and salt. Add dissolved gelatin and mix well. Stir in turkey, celery, apple, and onion. Turn into 1½-qt mold. Chill 10 to 15 minutes or until almost set. Meanwhile, soften 1 envelope gelatin in remaining 1/2 cup cold water. Stir over low heat until dissolved. Mash cranberry sauce with fork and stir in gelatin. Chill until mixture mounds slightly. Spoon on top of turkey mixture. Chill until firm.

Serves 8.

Smoked Chicken Surprise

2 envelopes unflavored gelatin
1/2 cup cold water
2½ cups buttermilk, divided
1 can (8½ oz) crushed pineapple
1/4 cup lemon juice
Salt to taste
1 tsp prepared mustard
2 cups smoked chicken, chopped
1 cup celery, chopped
1/4 cup unblanched almonds, chopped
2 tbsp pimiento, chopped
1½ tbsp minced onion
Lettuce leaves

Sprinkle gelatin over water to soften. In a 2-qt saucepan heat 1 cup buttermilk and gelatin over low heat, stirring constantly, until gelatin is dissolved. Add remaining buttermilk, pineapple with syrup, lemon juice, salt, and mustard. Chill until partially set. Fold in chicken, celery, almonds, pimiento, and onion. Pour into 7-cup salad mold; chill until firm. Unmold onto lettuce leaves.

Serves 8.

To get the most juice from a lemon, heat in a 300-degree oven for 5 minutes; refrigerate. Roll the lemon between the palms of your hands until soft. You will have about one-third more juice.

Oriental-Style Smoked Turkey Salad with Pears

3 cups smoked turkey
1 can (5 oz) water chestnuts, drained
1/4 cup green onion, chopped
1/2 cup celery, diced
3 fresh pears
Lemon juice

Cut turkey in julienne strips; slice water chestnuts. Combine turkey with water chestnuts, onion, and celery. Pile into salad bowl and place pear slices over mixture; sprinkle with lemon juice. Serve with a dressing made by combining 3/4 cup orange-flavored yogurt, 2 tbsp soy sauce, and 1/4 tsp powdered ginger.

For one-bowl salad, dice pears and toss with remaining ingredients, coating lightly with dressing.

Serves 6.

Smoked Chicken Salad

1 cup smoked chicken, diced
1 cup French dressing
1/2 cup sliced pineapple, drained
1/2 cup celery, diced
1/2 tsp minced onion
2 tbsp almonds, toasted, shredded
2 tbsp mayonnaise
Lettuce leaves

Marinate smoked chicken in French dressing for one hour or longer. Drain if necessary. Add pineapple, celery, onion, and almonds with just enough mayonnaise to moisten. Chill. Serve on lettuce leaves and garnish with additional shredded almonds.

Serves 4.

Fruity Smoked Chicken Salad

1 orange
15 large grapes
15 almonds, sliced
1 banana, sliced
1 apple, diced
3 cups smoked chicken, diced
1 cup mayonnaise
Lettuce leaves

Remove seeds and membrane from orange sections; cut sections in half. Cut grapes in half, removing seeds. Mix all ingredients lightly but thoroughly. Serve on lettuce leaves.

Serves 6 to 8.

Smoked Chicken Liver Salad

1 cup smoked chicken livers, diced
2 tbsp butter
Basic Seasoning or salt and pepper to
  taste
1 head lettuce
1/2 bunch curly endive
4 scallions, chopped
1/2 cup Roquefort or blue cheese,
  crumbled
2 hard-cooked eggs, chopped
1/3 cup French dressing

Sauté the chicken livers in butter and seasoning until lightly browned; chill; cut into pieces. Tear the lettuce and endive into bite-size pieces; add the chicken livers, scallions, cheese, and eggs. Toss with French dressing.

Serves 4 to 6.

Chicken and Pineapple Salad

1 envelope unflavored gelatin
1½ cups chicken stock or bouillon,
  divided
Salt to taste
2 tbsp lemon juice
1 can (13¼ oz) crushed pineapple,
  drained (reserve syrup)
1½ cups smoked chicken, diced
1/2 cup celery, diced
Lettuce leaves

Soften gelatin in 1/2 cup cold chicken stock; cook in 1 cup hot chicken stock and stir until gelatin is dissolved. Add salt, lemon juice, and 1/4 cup pineapple syrup. Chill to consistency of unbeaten egg white. Fold in smoked chicken, pineapple, and celery. Turn into 3-cup mold or individual molds and chill until firm. Unmold on lettuce leaves and serve with salad dressing.

Serves 4 to 6.

Smoked Chicken and Corn Salad

3 cups smoked chicken, diced
2 cups cooked whole kernel corn, drained
4 tomatoes, peeled, cubed
2 green peppers, chopped
2 cups mayonnaise, divided
Basic Seasoning or salt and pepper to
  taste
Lettuce leaves

Mix chicken, corn, tomatoes, and peppers. Stir in 1½ cups mayonnaise; season to taste. Serve on lettuce and garnish with remaining mayonnaise.

Serves 8.

*Country Smoked
Chicken Loaf*

*Chicken or
Turkey à la King*

Smoked Turkey Pasty

*Smoked Turkey
Club Sandwich with
Whole Smoked Turkey*

*Pickled
Smoked Seafood*

Smoked Rabbit
and Macaroni
with Salad Plate

Baked Smoked Squirrel Loaf

Pasty Plate

Pear and Smoked Chicken Salad

4 pears
Lemon juice
2 cups smoked chicken
3/4 cup celery, diced
1/4 cup green pepper, diced
2 tbsp parsley, minced
2 tbsp green onion, diced
Blue cheese dressing
Lettuce leaves

Peel and core pears; slice into wedges; sprinkle with lemon juice. Combine smoked chicken, celery, green pepper, parsley, and green onion. Add enough blue cheese dressing to moisten ingredients. Line individual salad bowls with greens. Place a mound of chicken salad in center of each; arrange pear wedges, spoke fashion, around smoked chicken salad.

Serves 6.

Smoked Chicken and Sweetbread Salad

1½ cups sweetbreads, precooked, diced
1½ cups smoked chicken, diced
1½ cups celery, diced
Salt to taste
3/4 cup mayonnaise
2 tbsp stuffed olives, chopped
2 tbsp chili sauce
2 tsp lemon juice
Lettuce

Have all ingredients chilled. Combine sweetbreads, chicken, celery, and salt. Combine mayonnaise with olives, chili sauce, and lemon juice; add to meat mixture and toss lightly. Serve on crisp lettuce on individual salad plates.

Serves 5 to 6.

Brains and sweetbreads are soft, white, very delicate in flavor, and require special care in preparation. They are unusually perishable, and should never be stored without precooking. To precook sweetbreads or brains, soak them for 15 minutes in cold water; then carefully remove the thin membranous covering to retain the original form. Cover with cold water to which 1 teaspoon salt and 1 tablespoon lemon juice or vinegar is added for each quart of water, and simmer 15 minutes. Then drain and place into cold water just long enough to chill quickly. The lemon juice or vinegar helps to keep the meat white. The meat is now thoroughly cooked and may be used a variety of ways.

Sweetbreads are often creamed with chicken, mushrooms, or veal, or they may be used in salads or browned in butter by broiling or pan-broiling. Precooked brains are often broken into pieces and scrambled with eggs, or dipped in egg and crumbs and fried in deep or shallow fat until delicately browned, or dipped in melted butter and broiled. They may also be reheated in a well-seasoned cream sauce or tomato sauce, or used to make soup.

Smoked Chicken Salad with Olives

1 tbsp lemon juice
3/4 cup mayonnaise
1/2 cup Spanish green olives, sliced
2 cups cooked elbow macaroni, drained
2 cups smoked chicken, diced
1 cup celery, diced
2 small onions, sliced
3/4 cup toasted almonds, sliced
Dash pepper
6 lettuce cups

Add lemon juice to mayonnaise, blending well. Combine with remaining ingredients, mixing lightly; chill. Serve in individual lettuce cups; garnish with additional sliced olives.

Serves 6 to 8.

Smoked Chicken Salad Mold

2 cups smoked chicken
1 cup celery, chopped
1 cup white grapes, halved
2 tbsp parsley, minced
Basic Seasoning or salt and pepper to
   taste
1½ tsp unflavored gelatin
1/4 cup cold water
1/2 cup chicken stock, heated
1 cup mayonnaise
1 cup whipping cream

Mix together chicken, celery, grapes, and parsley; season to taste. Soften gelatin in water and dissolve in hot chicken stock; stir into the chicken mixture. Combine mayonnaise with cream and fold in. Pour into 6- to 8-cup mold or 6 individual molds.

Serves 6.

Smoked Turkey and Tomato Mold

2 envelopes unflavored gelatin
1 can (10½ oz) consommé, divided
1 can (17½ oz) tomato juice
2 tbsp lemon juice
1/2 tsp tabasco sauce
2 cups smoked turkey
1 cup celery, chopped
1/2 cup cucumber, chopped
1/2 cup stuffed olives, chopped

Sprinkle gelatin over 1 cup consommé to soften. Place over boiling water and stir until gelatin is dissolved. Add remaining consommé, tomato juice, lemon juice, and tabasco. Chill until mixture is slightly thicker than unbeaten egg white. Fold in turkey, celery, cucumber, and olives. Turn into 8- to 10-cup mold. Chill until firm.

Serves 8 to 10.

Smoked Chicken Salad Hawaii

1¼ cups smoked chicken, diced
1/2 cup celery, diced
3/4 cup apples, diced
1½ tsp capers
1 cup mayonnaise, divided
1 head lettuce
16 small or 8 large pineapple slices
24 carrot sticks, 3 inches long
3 medium tomatoes
16 olives

Combine chicken, celery, apple, and capers. Moisten with mayonnaise. For each serving arrange a mound of the mixture in the center of crisp lettuce leaves. Top each with 2 small pineapple slices with carrot sticks inserted through centers (or place mound on top of large pineapple slice). Garnish with tomatoes cut in eighths, olives, and remaining mayonnaise.

Serves 8.

Chef's Salad

1 head lettuce
1 cup julienne strips smoked chicken
1/2 cup julienne strips celery
1 cup julienne strips Swiss cheese
2 tomatoes, peeled, quartered
1 can (4 oz) artichoke hearts
2 hard-cooked eggs, quartered
1/4 cup Thousand Island dressing
1/4 cup French dressing

Tear lettuce into bite-size pieces and toss with remaining ingredients, except the eggs and dressings. Garnish with eggs and pour over a mixture of the two dressings.

Serves 4.

Greens for salads should be refrigerated at least 24 hours after washing and draining. Then break or tear into small pieces. Head lettuce should be cut into quarters and then broken apart. Do not break until ready to use.

Smoked Turkey Salad with Tomatoes

2 cups smoked turkey, diced
1/2 cup peanuts, chopped
1 cup celery, diced
1 can (14½ oz) sliced cherry tomatoes or
   2 cups fresh, sliced
1/2 cup mayonnaise
Basic Seasoning or salt and pepper to
   taste
1/8 tsp tarragon
Lettuce leaves

Mix together the smoked turkey, nuts, celery, and tomatoes. Blend mayonnaise, seasoning, and tarragon. Fold mayonnaise mixture into turkey mixture; chill. Serve on lettuce leaves.

Serves 6.

Tomatoes Stuffed with Smoked Chicken Salad

1 cup smoked chicken, diced
3 tbsp cucumber, diced
1 cup mayonnaise, divided
1 cup cooked peas
3 hard-cooked eggs, chopped
2/3 cup celery, diced
3 tbsp French dressing
8 medium tomatoes

Mix all ingredients, except tomatoes, using only enough mayonnaise to moisten, and chill at least 30 minutes. Wash and peel tomatoes; cut out blossom end and cut tomatoes from top to within 1/4 inch of bottom into 5 or 6 wedge-shaped sections. Dash with salt and chill. Pull wedges apart to resemble petals of a flower and fill with salad which has been mixed with remaining mayonnaise.

Serves 8.

Chef's Salad Bowl

2 heads Boston lettuce
1 cup julienne strips smoked chicken
1 cup radishes, sliced
1 cup julienne strips baked ham
1 cup julienne strips Swiss cheese
1 cucumber, peeled, diced
1/2 bunch watercress
2 tomatoes, peeled
1/4 cup French dressing

Tear lettuce into a salad bowl. Add chicken, radishes, ham, cheese, and cucumber. Tuck in watercress and place tomato wedges around the rim. Add French dressing; toss at table.

Serves 6 to 8.

All tossed green salads should be served cold. For extra crispness, place salad plates and salad dressing under refrigeration several hours before mixing and serving.

Sandwiches and Sandwich Fillings

Smoked Chicken Liver Filling

1 cup onion, chopped
1/3 cup butter or margarine
1 lb smoked chicken livers, sliced
2 tbsp parsley, chopped
1 cup mushrooms, sliced
1 tbsp dry sherry
Basic Seasoning or salt and pepper to
   taste
1/3 cup half and half cream
Toast

Sauté onion in butter until brown. Add remaining ingredients except toast and cook over low heat 25 to 30 minutes or until thickened. Serve on hot buttered slices of toast as an open-face sandwich.

Serves 4 to 6.

Smoked Turkey Club Sandwiches

18 slices hot toast
1/4 cup mayonnaise
12 smoked turkey slices
6 lettuce leaves
3 small tomatoes, sliced
1 tbsp chili sauce
12 slices crisp bacon
6 stuffed olives
6 sweet pickles

Spread 6 slices of toast with mayonnaise; cover each with 2 slices of turkey and a lettuce leaf. Cover with a second slice of toast. Arrange tomato on top; spread with chili sauce, then 2 strips of bacon. Cover with third slice of toast. Cut diagonally and garnish with olives and pickles.

Makes 6.

Open-Face Smoked Turkey Supper Sandwiches

1 can (4½ oz) deviled ham
4 slices hot toast
4 large slices smoked turkey
1 can (10½ oz) cream of mushroom soup
3 tbsp mayonnaise
1/4 cup dry sherry
Paprika

Spread deviled ham on toast; top with turkey. Place in shallow baking pan. Dilute soup with mayonnaise and wine; heat to simmering, and spoon over sandwiches. Bake in 400-degree oven 10 minutes or until hot. Dust with paprika; serve at once.

Serves 4.

Superb Smoked Chicken Liver Filling

1 medium onion, chopped
1 tbsp butter or margarine
1/2 lb smoked chicken livers, diced
2 hard-cooked eggs, chopped
4 to 5 sticks celery, chopped
Salad oil
Basic Seasoning or salt and pepper to
taste

Sauté onion in butter until brown; cool. Mix together onion, finely diced smoked livers, eggs, and celery; add salad oil to make a spreading consistency. Season to taste.

Makes 5 or 6 sandwiches.

Smoked Chicken and Walnuts

1 cup smoked chicken, minced
1/3 cup celery, minced
1/4 cup walnuts, chopped
2 tbsp stuffed olives, minced
Mayonnaise

Combine all ingredients with enough mayonnaise to make a spreading consistency.

Makes 5 or 6 sandwiches.

Soups

Hearty Smoked Turkey Soup

2 tbsp onion, chopped
1/4 cup butter or margarine
1 tsp curry powder
1 cup raw potatoes, diced
1/2 cup carrots, diced
1/2 cup celery, sliced
3 cups turkey broth
Basic Seasoning or salt and pepper to
　　taste
1/2 pkg (9 oz) frozen French-style string
　　beans
1 cup smoked turkey, diced
1 tsp oregano
1 tbsp parsley, minced
1 can (14½ oz) evaporated milk
2 tbsp flour

Sauté the onion in butter in a large saucepan on top of the stove until transparent. Stir in the curry powder and cook a minute or two longer. Stir in potatoes, carrots, celery, broth, and seasoning to taste; bring to a boil. Simmer 10 to 15 minutes. Stir in green beans, turkey, oregano, and parsley. Combine milk and flour and stir in gently until well blended. Continue cooking until vegetables are crisp-tender. Adjust seasonings.

Serves 4 to 6.

Smoked Capon Soup

2 tbsp butter
1/4 cup almonds, slivered
1/4 cup green pepper, minced
1/4 cup green onions, sliced with tops
1 cup celery, thinly sliced
4 cups broth
1 cup smoked capon, diced
Basic Seasoning or salt and pepper to
　　taste
Chopped parsley

Melt butter in saucepan. Add almonds, green pepper, onions, and celery; sauté, stirring, about 5 minutes. Add broth and bring to boil. Add smoked capon and seasoning. Sprinkle with parsley.

Makes 5 cups.

Smoked Turkey Gobbler Soup

2 cups fresh tomatoes
1/2 cup celery, chopped
1 small onion, chopped
2 chicken bouillon cubes in 1 cup water
1/4 tsp pepper
1/4 cup butter
1/4 cup flour
4 cups milk, scalded
Salt to taste
1½ cups smoked turkey

In saucepan cook tomatoes, celery, onion, bouillon, and pepper for about 15 minutes. Melt butter in saucepan; blend in flour, then milk and cook until smooth and thickened. Add salt, vegetable mixture, and turkey. Heat to serving temperature.

Serves 5 to 6.

Curried Chicken Soup

1 medium onion, minced
1 tart apple, peeled, chopped
1/4 cup butter or margarine
2 cups smoked chicken, chopped
3 cups chicken broth
1 tbsp curry powder
Basic Seasoning or salt and pepper to taste
1/4 cup raisins
1/4 tsp dried thyme
1/4 cup peanuts, chopped
1 cup cooked rice

Sauté the onion and apple in butter in a heavy saucepan until onion is transparent. Add remaining ingredients, except peanuts and rice; cover and bake in 350-degree oven for 30 minutes. When ready to serve stir in the peanuts and adjust seasonings. Put 1/4 cup hot rice in each soup bowl and ladle soup into each.

Serves 4.

Curried Smoked Turkey Soup

1 cup celery, diced
1 cup apple, peeled, diced
1/2 cup onion, chopped
1/4 cup butter
1/4 cup flour
2 tsp curry powder
Basic Seasoning or salt and pepper to taste
1 qt milk, scalded
2 cups smoked turkey or chicken, diced

In skillet sauté celery, apple, and onion in butter until onion and apple are tender but not brown. Blend in flour, curry powder, and seasoning to taste. Add milk; cook, stirring constantly, until slightly thickened. Add turkey; heat to serving temperature.

Makes 6 to 8 cups.

Variations: Use different seasonings, vegetables, leftover meat, and/or broth.

Smoked Chicken Bisque

3 cups chicken stock, divided
1 cup smoked chicken, cubed
2 tbsp butter
2 tbsp flour
Basic Seasoning or salt and pepper to
taste
1 cup milk, scalded

Put 1½ cups chicken stock into blender container. Add chicken, butter, flour, and seasoning. Cover and process on high speed until smooth. Pour into saucepan. Stir in remaining 1½ cups stock. Cook over low heat 10 minutes. Add scalded milk. Serve hot. (Do not boil the bisque after the milk is added.)

Serves 4.

A leaf of lettuce dropped into a pot will absorb the grease from the top of the soup. Remove the lettuce and throw away as soon as it has served its purpose.

Delicacies

Smoked Turkey Supreme

2 lb fresh asparagus
2 tbsp butter
2 tbsp flour
1 cup milk, scalded
Salt to taste
1/4 tsp Worcestershire sauce
Dash tabasco sauce
1/2 cup cheese, grated
8 thin slices smoked turkey
1/4 cup almonds, slivered

Cook asparagus until just tender. In skillet melt butter and blend in flour. Add milk, salt, Worcestershire, and tabasco; cook and stir until thickened. Blend in cheese and stir until it melts. Arrange turkey slices in bottom of baking dish; top with drained asparagus. Pour cheese sauce over all. Place under broiler and heat until lightly browned. Sprinkle with almonds and serve at once.

Serves 4 to 6.

Smoked Chicken Liver and Anchovy Paste on Toast

5 smoked chicken livers
3 tbsp anchovy paste
3 tbsp butter
1/8 tsp pepper
Salt
4 egg yolks, divided
8 slices hot toast
1⅓ cups cream or evaporated milk

Make a paste of livers and anchovy paste. Add butter, pepper, dash of salt, and 1 egg yolk. Spread on toast and place under preheated broiler for 1 minute. Make a sauce by cooking remaining 3 egg yolks, dash of salt, and cream in top of double boiler over hot, not boiling, water about 10 minutes. Pour sauce over toast and serve.

Serves 8.

Apples with Smoked Chicken Stuffing

1¼ cups smoked chicken, minced
2 tbsp melted butter
4 large cooking apples, cored
4 whole cloves
1 tbsp toasted bread crumbs
1 tbsp sugar

Mix chicken with melted butter; fill center of each apple with chicken mixture and one clove. Place on shallow baking pan; sprinkle with bread crumbs and sugar; dot with additional butter. Bake at 350 degrees until soft but not mushy.

Serves 4.

Smoked Chicken or Turkey Potato Cakes

2 cups mashed potatoes*
2 tbsp onion, minced
2 cups smoked chicken
1 tbsp parsley, chopped
1/4 tsp tabasco sauce
2 tsp monosodium glutamate
1/4 tsp leaf thyme
Salt to taste
3 tbsp butter or margarine

Combines all ingredients, except butter. Shape into 8 flat cakes. Melt butter in skillet; add cakes; brown well on both sides.

Serves 4.

*If one package (4 servings) of instant mashed potatoes is used, reduce liquid called for by 1/2 cup.

Spaghetti with Smoked Chicken Livers

1 pkg (8 oz) spaghetti
2½ cups cooked tomatoes
1 clove garlic, chopped
2 tsp celery salt
1/2 tsp ginger
Basic Seasoning or salt and pepper to
    taste
1 tsp sugar
Dash cayenne pepper
1 cup beef stock
1 cup smoked chicken livers, chopped
1 cup mushrooms, sliced
4 tbsp fat
2 tbsp flour
1/2 cup Parmesan cheese, grated

Cook spaghetti in boiling salted water until tender; drain. Combine tomatoes and seasonings; cook together slowly for 30 minutes. Add stock. Sauté chopped livers and sliced mushrooms in fat until tender. Add flour and tomato mixture. Cook slowly for 15 minutes; then add to spaghetti; sprinkle with cheese.

Serves 6.

Variation: One cup diced smoked chicken may be used in place of livers.

Smoked Chicken Enchiladas

1 cup biscuit mix
1¼ cups water, divided
1 clove garlic, minced
1 tbsp olive oil
2 cans (8 oz ea) tomato sauce
1½ tsp chili powder
2 cups smoked chicken, diced
3/4 cup ripe olives, chopped
4 tbsp onion, chopped
1/2 cup sharp American cheese, grated,
    divided

Enchiladas are glorified tortillas; so first make the tortillas. Mix biscuit mix and 1/4 cup water; knead about 1 minute on cloth-covered board lightly dusted with flour. Shape into 8 balls; roll each into 5-inch circle. Lightly bake on ungreased griddle. Cool between folds of damp towel to prevent drying. To prepare sauce, sauté the garlic in olive oil; add tomato sauce, 1 cup water, and chili powder; heat thoroughly. Brush the cooled tortillas on both sides with melted butter. Cover each with a portion of smoked chicken, olives, onion, and cheese. Roll up; place close together in greased shallow 8-inch-square baking dish. Pour sauce over rolls; sprinkle with remaining onion and cheese. Bake 15 minutes or until hot and bubbly.

Serves 4.

Smoked Duck Meatballs

2 cups smoked duck, ground
1/2 cup dry bread crumbs
1 tbsp instant dried onion
1/2 cup milk
1 egg, beaten
Basic Seasoning or salt and pepper to
   taste
1/4 tsp monosodium glutamate
1 tbsp shortening
1 can (6 oz) mushrooms
Water
2 bouillon cubes
1/4 cup flour
1 cup sour cream
4 cups cooked noodles
Paprika

Mix together ground duck, crumbs, onion, milk, egg, and seasonings. Shape into 1½-inch balls. Melt shortening in heavy skillet over medium heat and brown duck meatballs on all sides. Cover skillet, lower heat, and cook 10 minutes. Meanwhile, combine mushroom liquid with enough hot water to make 1 cup; add bouillon cubes and stir to dissolve. Remove meat from skillet with slotted spoon and keep warm. Blend flour into pan drippings. Add prepared mushroom liquid; stir and cook until well-blended and thick. Stir in sour cream and mushrooms. Heat through. To serve, arrange duck meatballs on bed of hot cooked noodles. Top with sour cream sauce. Sprinkle with paprika.

Serves 4 to 6.

To prevent the contents of casserole dishes from splattering the glass cover, apply the pure vegetable spray-on coating which prevents food from sticking to all types of cookware to the inside of the lid.

For a clear gravy, use cornstarch, potato starch, or arrowroot as thickeners. Flour makes an opaque gravy.

Do not throw away any wine that has turned to vinegar; use it in the same way as any commercial wine vinegar.

To soften marshmallows, place them in a plastic bag and immerse in hot water for a few minutes.

One teaspoon of lemon juice boiled with rice will make the rice whiter.

Chapter 3

Smoke-roasted Wild Game

Casseroles and Baked Dishes

Smoked Venison and Noodles

1/2 pkg (16 oz) medium noodles
1 can (10 oz) frozen cream of shrimp
   soup
1 cup milk
Dash tabasco sauce
2 cups smoked venison, chopped
1 can (4 oz) mushroom crowns, drained
1 can (4 oz) pimiento, drained, diced
1 pkg (4 oz) corn chips, crushed

Cook noodles in boiling, salted water according to package directions; drain. Combine soup, milk, and tabasco in saucepan; cook over low heat until bubbly. Gently mix noodles, soup mixture, smoked venison, mushrooms, and pimiento. Spoon half the smoked venison mixture into greased 2-qt casserole; sprinkle with half the crushed corn chips. Repeat with remaining venison mixture and corn chips. Bake in 350-degree oven 35 minutes or until bubbly.

Serves 4.

When cooking macaroni, noodles, rice, or spaghetti, add a little cooking oil to the cooking water. This not only reduces the chance of boiling over, but will keep these foods from sticking together.

Curried Smoked Mountain Sheep Loaf

2½ cups smoked mountain sheep, diced
1 small green pepper, sliced
1 cup fresh bread crumbs
1 cup green beans, cooked
1 envelope dehydrated onion soup mix
1¼ cups water
Basic Seasoning or salt and pepper to
   taste
1 to 1½ tsp curry powder
2 eggs, beaten
Mint jelly

Put smoked mountain sheep and green pepper through food grinder, using medium blade; combine with bread crumbs and green beans. Blend onion soup mix, water, seasoning, and curry powder in saucepan. Cover. Simmer 5 minutes; cool slightly. Combine soup mixture, smoked-sheep mixture, and eggs; blend well. Turn into greased 9 x 5 x 3-inch loaf pan. Bake at 350 degrees for 50 minutes or until meat is firm and well-browned on top. Serve with mint jelly.

Serves 6.

Smoked Venison One-Dish Meal

2 small onions, chopped
2 tbsp butter or margarine
2 cups smoked venison, chopped
1½ cups cooked rice
1½ cups canned tomatoes
2 cups canned corn
Basic Seasoning or salt and pepper to
   taste

Sauté onion in butter until brown; combine with remaining ingredients and pour into greased casserole. Bake in 350-degree oven 30 minutes or until heated through. During the last 5 minutes, top with shredded mozzarella or Jack cheese, if desired.

Serves 6 to 8.

Baked Smoked Squirrel Loaf

4 cups smoked squirrel, ground
1 cup milk
1 cup chicken stock
Salt to taste
1 small onion, minced
2 eggs, beaten
2 cups soft bread crumbs
2 medium tomatoes
1 tbsp parsley, minced

Mix all ingredients, except tomatoes and parsley. Stir well and pour into greased loaf pan. Bake in preheated 350-degree oven 1 hour or until firm and slightly browned. Unmold and serve hot or cold on platter garnished with sliced tomatoes and parsley.

Serves 6 to 8.

Smoked Rabbit Soufflé

4 tbsp butter or margarine
4 tbsp flour
2 cups milk, scalded
1/2 cup bread crumbs, grated
1 tbsp parsley, minced
1/4 tsp nutmeg, grated
Basic Seasoning or salt and pepper to
   taste
2 cups smoked rabbit, diced
3 eggs, separated, beaten

Melt butter in saucepan; stir in flour until smooth. Gradually add milk, stirring until it boils and thickens. Remove from heat and stir in bread crumbs. Mix together the parsley, nutmeg, seasoning, and smoked rabbit; stir into sauce mixture. Stir a little hot mixture into the beaten egg yolks, then stir into remaining sauce. Fold in stiffly beaten egg whites. Turn the rabbit mixture into a heated greased baking dish and bake in 350-degree oven 45 minutes to 1 hour. Serve with a cream gravy, if desired.

Serves 4 to 6.

Smoked Rabbit Tamale Pie

4½ cups water
1½ tsp salt
1½ cups cornmeal
1 cup ripe olives, chopped
1/2 cup onion, chopped
1/2 clove garlic, crushed
1/2 cup green pepper, chopped
1/4 cup celery, chopped
5 tbsp butter or margarine, divided
1 tsp chili powder
1 can (8 oz) tomato sauce
Salt to taste
1/2 tsp basil leaf, crumbled
1/2 tsp Worcestershire sauce
2 cups smoked rabbit, chopped

Bring water and 1½ tsp salt to boiling. Slowly add cornmeal, stirring constantly. Cover; cook slowly 20 minutes, stirring occasionally. Add olives. Cover; set aside to cool. Sauté onion, garlic, green pepper, and celery in 3 tbsp butter. Add chili powder, tomato sauce, salt to taste, basil, and Worcestershire; simmer. Add smoked rabbit; remove from heat. Spread two-thirds of cornmeal on bottom and sides of buttered 2-qt casserole. Add rabbit mixture. Spoon remaining cornmeal mixture on top. Brush with 2 tbsp melted butter. Bake in 400-degree oven for 30 minutes. Place under broiler a few minutes for a crisp top.

Serves 6.

Smoked Rabbit Macaroni Casserole

4 tbsp butter or margarine
4 tbsp flour
Basic Seasoning or salt and pepper to
  taste
1 tsp dry mustard
Dash of cayenne
1 tsp Worcestershire sauce
Dash of tabasco sauce
1 can (4 oz) mushrooms, sliced
Chicken broth, heated
1½ cups milk, scalded
2 cups smoked rabbit, diced
2 cups cooked macaroni shells
1/4 cup ripe olives, sliced
4 slices (4 oz) American cheese

Melt butter in saucepan; blend in flour, seasonings, Worcestershire, and tabasco. Drain and reserve mushrooms. Measure liquid; add sufficient chicken broth to make 1½ cups. Gradually stir into flour mixture; add milk. Cook over medium heat, stirring constantly, until mixture thickens and comes to boil; remove from heat. Add smoked rabbit, macaroni, olives, and reserved mushrooms. Turn half the mixture into greased 1½-qt casserole; dice two slices cheese and add. Top with remaining macaroni mixture. Cut remaining cheese slices into triangles; arrange in pattern on top of casserole. Bake in 425-degree oven 15 to 20 minutes until browned and bubbly.

Serves 6.

Smoked Venison Loaf

4 cups smoked venison, ground
2 eggs, beaten
10 crackers, crushed
1 tsp dried sweet basil, crushed
1/2 cup canned milk
2 hard-cooked eggs, diced
1/2 tsp pepper, coarsely ground
1 can (8 oz) tomato sauce
1 tsp Worcestershire sauce

Mix smoked venison thoroughly with eggs and crackers; add basil, milk, hard-cooked eggs, and pepper. Place on a greased cooky sheet and form into a loaf. Mix together tomato sauce and Worcestershire; pour over loaf. Bake 45 minutes in 350-degree oven. Add water if necessary to keep moist.

Serves 4 to 6.

Oklahoma Squirrel Pie

2 cups chicken stock, divided
1⅓ cups flour, divided
2½ cups smoked squirrel, diced
1 cup potatoes, cooked, diced
3/4 cup peas, cooked
3/4 cup celery, diced
Salt to taste
1½ tsp baking soda
1/4 tsp salt
3 tbsp butter
1/3 cup milk

Make a paste by blending 1/2 cup cold chicken stock and 1/3 cup flour; add to remaining heated stock and cook over direct heat, stirring constantly, until sauce boils and thickens. Combine with smoked squirrel, potatoes, peas, and celery; season to taste and pour into greased casserole. Sift together 1 cup flour, baking soda, and salt. Cut in butter with pastry blender. Add milk and stir until dough just stiffens. Turn onto a floured board and roll to 1/4-inch thickness; cut to fit over casserole mixture. Bake in preheated 425-degree oven about 20 minutes or until brown.

Serves 6 to 8.

Smoked Venison in Barbecue Sauce

4 cups smoked venison, sliced
1 cup catsup
1 medium onion, sliced
1 clove garlic, diced
1/2 cup beer
1 can (8 oz) tomato sauce
Basic Seasoning or salt and pepper to taste
Buttered sandwich buns

Place smoked venison in baking dish. Combine remaining ingredients, except sandwich buns; mix well and pour over smoked venison. Cover and bake at 300 degrees for about 45 minutes. Serve hot over heated sandwich buns.

Serves 6 to 8.

Onions with Smoked Rabbit Stuffing

6 large red Italian or Spanish onions
Salt
2 slices bacon, diced
1 cup smoked rabbit, minced
1 egg, slightly beaten
1/2 cup herb-seasoned bread stuffing
2 tbsp water
Basic Seasoning or salt and pepper to
   taste

Peel onions; cut slice off tops. Parboil onions in boiling salted water 20 to 30 minutes or until tender. Cut out centers to make shells about 1/2-inch thick; sprinkle insides with salt. Chop enough of centers to make 1/2 cup. Fry bacon; set aside. Sauté chopped onion in bacon fat until lightly browned. Combine minced smoked rabbit, egg, bread stuffing, water, seasoning, sautéed onion, and diced bacon. Stuff onions; place in shallow baking dish with small amount of water. Bake at 375 degrees for 30 minutes or until lightly browned.

Serves 6.

Smoked Venison Potato Pudding

2 cups smoked venison, ground
3 medium potatoes
1 small onion
3 tbsp butter or margarine
3/4 cup hot milk
2 eggs, beaten
1 small bay leaf
Basic Seasoning or salt and pepper to
   taste

Grind meat, potatoes, and onion and mix together; melt butter in hot milk. Add to remaining ingredients and blend well. Pour into greased baking dish and set in pan of water; bake in preheated 350-degree oven 1 hour or until set. Serve with a rich brown gravy, if desired.

Serves 4 to 6.

Applesauce Moose Loaf

1½ lb (2½ cups) smoked moose, ground
3/4 cup quick or old-fashioned oats,
   uncooked
3/4 cup canned applesauce
Basic Seasoning or salt and pepper to
   taste
1 egg, beaten
Cheese for garnish

Preheat oven to 350 degrees. Combine all ingredients thoroughly in a large bowl. Pack firmly into greased 8½ x 4½ x 2½-inch loaf pan. Bake about 1 hour. Dot with cheese triangles; let stand 5 minutes before slicing.

Smoked Venison Casserole

2 cups cooked small elbow macaroni
1 cup smoked venison, chopped
Basic Seasoning or salt and pepper to
  taste
1 tsp pimiento, sliced
1/4 cup green pepper, sliced
Cheddar cheese slices
Cornflake crumbs
2 tbsp butter or margarine
Lemon wedges
Sweet pickle
Carrot strips
Celery sticks
Italian garlic breadsticks

Lightly mix the cooked macaroni and smoked venison. Add seasoning, pimiento, and green pepper. Put into a well-greased casserole. Place sliced cheese on top; sprinkle on a layer of cornflake crumbs and dot with butter. Bake in 300-degree oven for about 30 minutes or until heated through. Serve with lemon, pickle, carrots, celery, and breadsticks.

Serves 4.

Smoked Mountain Sheep Loaf

1/2 cup catsup
1 can (10½ oz) beef broth
1 tsp Worcestershire sauce
1/2 tsp sugar
1/4 cup plus 2 tbsp butter or margarine,
  divided
1/2 cup onion, chopped
1 pkg (8 oz) herb-flavored bread stuffing
  mix, divided
1/2 cup carrots, grated
1/4 cup green pepper, diced
1/4 cup water
1½ lb (2½ cups) smoked mountain sheep,
  ground
1 egg
Salt to taste

Combine catsup, beef broth, Worcestershire, sugar, and 2 tbsp butter in small saucepan; cook over medium heat until mixture comes to a boil. Remove from heat; reserve. Sauté onion in 1/4 cup butter in skillet until softened; mix well with 1/2 pkg of stuffing mix, carrot, green pepper, and water. In bowl combine remaining stuffing mix, smoked mountain sheep, egg, salt, and 1/2 cup reserved catsup mixture; mix well. Press half the meat mixture into 9 x 5 x 2-inch loaf pan. Press stuffing mixture firmly over meat layer; press remaining meat mixture carefully over stuffing layer; turn loaf out onto baking pan. Bake in 350-degree oven for 1 hour, brushing loaf with remaining catsup mixture several times.

Serves 6.

Smoked Squirrel Pie with Curried Potatoes

1/2 cup melted butter or margarine, divided
3 tbsp flour
1/2 tsp salt
1/2 tsp leaf rosemary, crumbled
1½ cups chicken broth, heated
1/2 cup light cream, scalded
2 cups smoked squirrel, diced
1 can (4 oz) mushrooms, sliced, drained
3/4 cup cooked peas
1/2 pkg (4 servings) instant mashed potatoes
1 egg, beaten
1 tsp curry powder

Heat 3 tbsp butter in saucepan. Stir in flour, salt, and rosemary; gradually stir in chicken broth. Cook, stirring constantly, until mixture thickens. Stir in cream, smoked squirrel, mushrooms, and peas; spoon into baking dishes. Prepare potatoes according to package directions; beat in egg, curry powder, and 3 tbsp melted butter. Spoon around edges of dishes; pour remaining butter over potatoes. Bake in 350-degree oven for 15 to 20 minutes or until potatoes are browned.

Serves 6.

Southern Smoked Squirrel

1/4 cup onion, chopped
3 tbsp butter or margarine
1/4 cup flour
2 chicken bouillon cubes
1 tsp onion salt
1½ cups milk, scalded
1 tsp Worcestershire sauce
1 tbsp prepared mustard
4 cups smoked squirrel, diced
1 cup cooked vegetables, drained
1 pkg (15 oz) corn bread mix

Sauté onion in butter until soft; blend in flour, chicken bouillon cubes, and onion salt. Slowly stir in milk; add Worcestershire and mustard. Cook over medium heat, stirring constantly, until mixture thickens and boils 1 minute. Add smoked squirrel and vegetables; turn into 2½-qt casserole. Prepare corn bread mix according to package directions. Spoon corn bread mixture over squirrel mixture. (If casserole is not large enough to take all the corn bread mixture, bake any remaining batter as muffins.) Bake in 400-degree oven for 25 to 30 minutes or until corn bread is golden brown and squirrel mixture is bubbly.

Hot Squirrel Casserole

1½ cups smoked squirrel, diced
1 cup celery, diced
1/2 cup walnuts, chopped
1/4 cup watercress, chopped
1 pimiento, chopped
2 tbsp lemon juice
2 tsp onion, minced
Basic Seasoning or salt and pepper to
    taste
1/2 cup mayonnaise
1/4 cup milk
2 tbsp Parmesan cheese, grated

Combine all ingredients, except cheese. Spoon into 4 individual baking dishes or 1 9-inch pie plate; sprinkle with cheese. Bake in 450-degree oven for 15 minutes until lightly browned.

Serves 4.

Oriental-Style Dishes

Smoked Rabbit with Chinese Vegetables

3/4 cup onion, sliced
2 tbsp butter or margarine
1 can (13 oz) chicken broth
1/4 cup water chestnuts, sliced
1 can (4 oz) mushrooms, drained, sliced
Basic Seasoning or salt and pepper to
    taste
1/2 tsp ground ginger
1 pkg frozen snow peas
2 cups smoked rabbit, chopped
2 tbsp cornstarch
2 tbsp water
Hot buttered rice

Sauté onion in butter until tender. Add chicken broth, water chestnuts, mushrooms, seasoning, and ginger; mix well. Add snow peas and smoked rabbit. Cover and simmer 2 minutes. Dissolve cornstarch in water; add to smoked rabbit mixture. Cook until sauce thickens. Serve on hot buttered rice.

Serves 6.

Chinese Smoked Rabbit Pie in Almond Crust

2½ cups chicken broth
1 cup celery, sliced
2 tbsp cornstarch
2 tbsp soy sauce
1/4 cup water
1/2 tsp ginger, ground
Basic Seasoning or salt and pepper to
    taste
2 cups smoked rabbit, diced
1 can (1 lb 4 oz) pineapple chunks,
    drained
1 cup small white onions, cooked
1/4 cup water chestnuts, sliced
1/3 cup blanched almonds, chopped,
    ground
1 pkg piecrust mix

Heat broth to boiling in saucepan. Add celery; simmer about 5 minutes until just tender. Combine cornstarch, soy sauce, water, ginger, and seasoning; stir into hot mixture. Cook, stirring constantly, until clear and slightly thickened. Add smoked rabbit, pineapple, onions, and water chestnuts; heat thoroughly. Turn into 2-qt casserole. Add almonds to piecrust mix; prepare according to package directions. Roll to fit top of casserole; place over hot rabbit mixture. Cut vents in pastry to allow steam to escape during baking. Bake at 425 degrees for 20 to 25 minutes or until crust is browned.

Serves 4 to 6.

To skin or blanch almonds drop them into boiling water, turn off flame, and let stand 3 minutes. Slip skins off and dry nuts on a clean dish towel.

Smoked Rabbit Chop Suey

1/4 cup mushrooms, sliced
2 tbsp butter or margarine
2 cups smoked rabbit, chopped
1 cup celery, diced
1 small carrot, diced
1 medium onion, diced
1½ cups chicken broth or bouillon
2 cups canned bean sprouts with liquid
3 tbsp cornstarch
3 tbsp soy sauce
1½ cups cooked rice

Sauté mushrooms in butter until lightly browned. Add rabbit, celery, carrot, onion, and broth. Cover and simmer 10 to 15 minutes until vegetables are tender. Add bean sprouts and liquid; heat to boiling. Mix cornstarch and soy sauce; add gradually to the boiling mixture, stirring constantly. Cook 2 minutes until slightly thickened. Serve over hot rice.

Serves 6 to 8.

If you cut your finger slightly while preparing dinner, put some flour on it to stop the bleeding.

Smoked Squirrel Far East

1/2 cup onion, chopped
2 tbsp butter or margarine
2 tbsp quick-cooking tapioca
1/2 tsp salt
1/2 tsp ground cinnamon
1/2 tsp ground ginger
1/8 tsp ground cloves
2½ cups chicken broth
8 whole cardamom seeds
1 tbsp whole coriander
1 tsp whole peppercorns
2 medium oranges
3 cups smoked squirrel, diced
1 large apple, diced
Cooked rice

Sauté onion in butter in large skillet until tender, but not brown. Combine tapioca, salt, cinnamon, ginger, and cloves; add to skillet. Add broth and whole spices tied in cheesecloth. Bring to a boil; simmer 15 minutes. Remove spice bag. Peel and section oranges, saving all the juice; stir into spice mixture. Add smoked squirrel and apple; simmer 10 minutes longer. Serve over hot rice.

Serves 4 to 6.

Smoked Rabbit Oriental

1 cup onion, sliced
1 large green pepper, seeded, cut in strips
4 tbsp butter or margarine
2 cans (3 to 4 oz ea) mushrooms
3 cups smoked rabbit, cubed
1½ cups celery, sliced
2½ cups chicken broth, divided
4 tbsp cornstarch
1/8 tsp pepper
3 tbsp soy sauce
4 ripe tomatoes, cut in wedges
2 cans (3 oz ea) Chinese noodles

Sauté onion and green pepper in butter in skillet 3 minutes. Drain mushrooms, reserving liquid; add mushrooms and smoked rabbit to skillet. Cook over low heat about 10 minutes; add celery. Mix 1/4 cup chicken broth with cornstarch to make a smooth paste. Add remaining chicken broth and reserved mushroom liquid to rabbit mixture. Cook until hot; stir in cornstarch mixture. Cook, stirring constantly, until sauce is bubbly and clear. Stir in pepper and soy sauce; add tomatoes. Cook slowly 5 to 10 minutes or until slightly thickened. Serve over Chinese noodles.

Serves 8.

Variation: Squirrel or wild turkey may be used in place of rabbit.

Creamed Dishes

Curried Venison, Seattle Style

1½ medium onions, minced
3 stalks celery, chopped
2 apples, minced
1/4 cup butter or margarine
2 tsp curry powder
1/8 tsp pepper
1/4 tsp ginger
1/4 tsp tabasco sauce
1/2 tbsp Worcestershire sauce
2 cups stock or bouillon
2 tbsp flour
1/4 cup cold water
3 cups smoked venison, cubed
1 cup whipping cream
1 egg yolk, beaten
Basic Seasoning or salt and pepper to taste
3 cups cooked rice

Sauté onions, celery, and apples in butter until slightly brown. Stir in curry powder and simmer 5 minutes. Add remaining seasonings and stock and cook 20 minutes. Stir in flour mixed with water and cook 5 minutes, stirring until thickened. Remove from heat and allow to stand at room temperature 1 hour. Reheat and add smoked venison; mix together cream and egg and add to cooled mixture. Season to taste. Heat to boiling point, stirring constantly. Serve on rice.

Serves 6 to 8.

Smoked Rabbit Supreme

2 cups half and half or light cream
1 bay leaf
1/4 cup onion, sliced
5 sprigs parsley
2 whole cloves
3 tbsp butter or margarine, melted
3 tbsp flour
Basic Seasoning or salt and pepper to taste
1 tbsp parsley, chopped
2 tbsp pimiento, diced
1 cup smoked rabbit, chopped
6 French rolls, scooped out, toasted or 6 baked potatoes

Heat cream, bay leaf, onion, parsley, and cloves to scalding. Remove from heat; strain. Blend butter and flour. Gradually add scalded mixture, stirring constantly. Heat until sauce thickens. Add seasoning, parsley, pimiento, and smoked rabbit; heat. Serve in buttered French rolls or over baked potatoes.

Serves 6.

Quick-on-the-Draw Smoked Elk Curry

2 cups smoked elk, diced
1/4 cup flour
Basic Seasoning or salt and pepper to
  taste
3 tbsp butter or margarine
1 medium onion, chopped
1½ tsp curry powder
3/4 cup light cream, heated
Corn bread or hominy grits

Roll smoked elk in flour and seasoning; sauté in melted butter; add onion and sauté until transparent. Add curry powder and cream, stirring over low heat 15 to 20 minutes until thickened and smooth. Serve over corn bread or hominy grits.

Serves 3 to 4.

Creamed Jerky on Toast

1/2 cup smoked venison jerky, ground
1/2 cup water
2 tbsp butter or margarine
2 tbsp flour
2 cups milk
4 slices buttered toast
Parsley

Place smoked jerky in water in saucepan and bring to a boil. Remove from heat and let stand for 1 hour. Melt butter in skillet; add flour, mixing well to form a smooth paste. Remove from heat and add milk, stirring constantly. When mixture is smooth, return to heat. Continue to stir; add more milk if necessary to make a medium-thick sauce. Add jerky with liquid, blending thoroughly. Simmer for about 10 minutes. Serve over buttered toast sprinkled with parsley.

Serves 4.

Creamed Smoked Rabbit

4 tbsp butter
4 tbsp flour
2 tsp onion juice
1 cup chicken consommé, heated
1/2 cup light cream, scalded
1/2 cup dry white wine
2 cups smoked rabbit, diced

Melt butter; blend in flour and add onion juice, chicken consommé, and cream. Simmer while stirring for 1 minute. Add wine and smoked rabbit. Bring to a simmer and serve on toast or in patty shells.

Serves 4.

Smoked Squirrel Almandine

1/2 lb mushrooms, sliced
1/3 cup green pepper, diced
4 tbsp butter or margarine
1/3 cup flour
2 cups chicken broth, heated
1 cup light cream
1/8 tsp nutmeg
Basic Seasoning or salt and pepper to taste
2 cups smoked squirrel, diced
3 tbsp dry sherry
1/3 cup pimiento, diced
1/2 cup blanched almonds, toasted
Patty shells or toast points

Sauté mushrooms and green pepper in butter 5 minutes. Add flour; blend until smooth. Stir in chicken broth, then the light cream. Add nutmeg, seasoning, and smoked squirrel; simmer 5 minutes. Add sherry and pimiento; sprinkle with almonds. Garnish with additional pimiento, if desired. Serve in patty shells or on toast points.

Serves 6 to 8.

Smoked Squirrel Supreme

4 tbsp butter or margarine
4 tbsp flour
2 cups chicken broth or bouillon, heated
2½ cups smoked squirrel, chopped
1/2 cup fresh button mushrooms
Basic Seasoning or salt and pepper to taste
1/4 tsp nutmeg, grated
2 egg yolks, beaten
1/2 cup light cream
Corn bread or hominy grits

Melt butter in a 2-qt saucepan over boiling water; stir in flour until smooth. Gradually add chicken broth, stirring until thickened. Add smoked squirrel, mushrooms, and seasonings. Steam, covered, until thoroughly heated, about 10 minutes. Beat egg yolks with cream and gradually stir into smoked-meat mixture just before serving; cook until thickened, about 10 minutes. Serve over corn bread or hominy grits.

Serves 6.

Creamed Smoked Rabbit with Egg Garnish

3½ tbsp butter or margarine
3½ tbsp flour
2½ cups milk, scalded
2½ cups smoked rabbit, chopped
Basic Seasoning or salt and pepper to taste
2 tsp lemon juice
1 tsp onion, grated
1 hard-cooked egg, chopped

Melt butter and blend in flour; add milk gradually and cook over very low heat, stirring frequently, until smooth and thick. Add smoked rabbit and heat thoroughly, stirring occasionally. Season to taste. Stir in lemon juice and onion. Serve over toast or baked potato, garnished with chopped egg.

Serves 4 to 6.

Smoked Rabbit à la King

1/3 cup celery, chopped
3 tbsp onion, chopped
3 tbsp green pepper, chopped
3 tbsp mushrooms, sliced
1/3 cup water
1/4 cup butter or margarine
1/4 cup flour
2½ cups milk, scalded
Basic Seasoning or salt and pepper to taste
2 cups smoked rabbit, chopped

Cook vegetables and mushrooms gently in water in a covered saucepan until just tender, about 20 minutes. Drain and reserve liquid. In skillet melt butter; blend in flour. Add vegetable liquid to milk and pour gradually into flour mixture, stirring constantly. Cook over low heat until thick and smooth; season to taste. Add vegetable-mushroom mixture and smoked rabbit to the sauce and heat thoroughly. Serve over hot biscuits.

Serves 4 to 6.

Curried Smoked Rabbit with Rice

2 cups chicken broth or bouillon
1/4 cup onion, chopped
1 clove garlic, halved
1 tsp curry powder
1/4 cup milk
1/3 cup flour
2 cups smoked rabbit, chopped
Basic Seasoning or salt and pepper to taste
1½ cups cooked rice

Simmer broth, onion, garlic, and curry powder in a covered pan for 20 minutes; remove garlic. Stir milk into flour; add a few tablespoonfuls of the hot broth; then stir mixture into remaining broth. Cook over low heat until thick and smooth, stirring frequently. Add rabbit and season to taste. Heat thoroughly and serve over hot rice.

Serves 4 to 6.

Smoked Rabbit Almandine

1 pkg (15 oz) corn bread mix
1/3 lb mushrooms, sliced
2 tbsp butter or margarine
1/4 cup flour
Basic Seasoning or salt and pepper to taste
Dash crumbled leaf thyme
2⅔ cups chicken broth, heated
1⅓ cups smoked rabbit, diced
1/4 cup dry sherry
1/3 cup blanched almonds, toasted

Prepare corn bread according to package directions. Sauté mushrooms in butter 5 minutes or until tender. Add flour and seasonings; mix well. Gradually add chicken broth. Cook until sauce thickens and simmer 5 minutes, stirring occasionally. Add rabbit and sherry. Heat well; adjust seasonings. Add almonds; serve on squares of hot buttered corn bread.

Serves 6 to 8.

Hash

Smoked Moose Hash

1 lb (2 cups) smoked moose
2 medium potatoes
1 medium onion
1 tsp oregano
1/2 tsp thyme
1/8 tsp cayenne pepper
Basic Seasoning or salt and pepper to
 taste
1 cup water
1 strip bacon, halved

Grind meat, potatoes and onion in meat grinder. Add remaining ingredients, except bacon; mix thoroughly. Place in a well-greased casserole; put bacon strips on top and bake in 400-degree oven for 1 hour.

Serves 4 to 6.

Baked Smoked Rabbit Hash

2 cups smoked rabbit, chopped
2 cups raw potatoes, chopped
2 tbsp green pepper, chopped
3/4 cup onion, chopped
Basic Seasoning or salt and pepper to
 taste
1/2 cup chicken broth or bouillon
1/4 cup buttered bread crumbs

Mix all ingredients, except the crumbs. Lightly pile into a greased baking dish. Cover and bake in 350-degree oven about 40 minutes. Remove cover and sprinkle crumbs on top. Bake, uncovered, 20 minutes longer to brown.

Serves 4 to 6.

Juneau-Style Smoked Bear Hash

2 cups smoked bear, diced
1/2 cup flour
Basic Seasoning or salt and pepper to
 taste
3 tbsp butter or margarine
1 cup onion, chopped
1 cup boiled potatoes, diced
1 tbsp vinegar
1 small bay leaf
1 tbsp celery tops, sliced

Dredge smoked bear in flour and seasoning; sauté in butter. Remove from skillet and sauté onion in same fat. When brown, remove onion and brown potatoes, adding more butter if needed. When potatoes are browned, remove and place with onions and meat in a large bowl. Add vinegar, bay leaf, and celery tops, blending thoroughly; return to skillet and let cook over low heat 30 minutes.

Serves 4.

Savory Smoked Squirrel Hash

2 cans (3 to 4 oz ea) mushrooms,
    chopped
4 cups smoked squirrel, chopped
4 cups potatoes, pared, chopped
1 large onion, chopped
1 green pepper, chopped
Basic Seasoning or salt and pepper to
    taste
1/3 cup butter or margarine
2 tbsp flour
1/2 tsp salt
1/8 tsp pepper
1/4 tsp poultry seasoning
1 cup chicken broth, heated
1 cup milk, scalded

Drain mushrooms. Reserve 4 tbsp mushrooms; discard liquid. Put remaining mushrooms, smoked squirrel, potatoes, onion, and green pepper through food grinder; stir in seasoning. Form mixture into 16 patties. Heat butter in large skillet. Cook patties over low heat about 10 minutes or until potatoes are partially cooked and crusty on bottom. Turn and repeat until potatoes are cooked. Remove to heated platter; keep warm. Blend flour into remaining fat in skillet; add salt, pepper, and poultry seasoning. Slowly stir in chicken broth and milk. Cook over medium heat, stirring constantly, until thickened and bubbly. Reduce heat; add reserved mushrooms and simmer 2 to 3 minutes. Serve sauce over patties.

Serves 8.

Pastry Dishes

Smoked Squirrel Biscuit Roll

1 cup smoked squirrel, chopped
1 can (4 oz) mushrooms, sliced, drained
2 tbsp pimiento, diced
2 tbsp parsley flakes
1 can (10½ oz) cream of mushroom
    soup, divided
2 cups biscuit mix
1 tsp onion powder
1/2 tsp salt
1⅓ cups milk, divided

Combine smoked squirrel, mushrooms, pimiento, parsley, and 2 tbsp undiluted soup in small bowl. Combine biscuit mix, onion powder, and salt in medium-size bowl. Add 2/3 cup milk; stir until moistened. Turn out on lightly floured surface; knead 5 or 6 times. Roll out dough to 9 x 12-inch rectangle. Spread smoked-squirrel mixture on dough. Roll up, jelly-roll fashion, starting at short side; place on greased cooky sheet. Bake in 425-degree oven for 20 to 25 minutes or until golden brown. Serve with sauce made by combining remaining soup with 2/3 cup milk. Heat slowly, stirring until smooth.

Serves 4 to 6.

Smoked Venison Biscuit Roll

Biscuit Dough

    2 cups flour
    1 tbsp baking powder
    1/2 tsp salt
    2 tbsp butter or margarine
    3/4 to 1 cup milk

Filling

    1 cup smoked venison, ground
    1/4 cup cream of mushroom soup
    1 tbsp bacon, cooked, crumbled
    Basic Seasoning or salt and pepper to
      taste
    1 tbsp onion, minced
    1 tsp parsley, minced
    Melted butter
    Sugar

Sift together flour, baking powder, and salt. Cut in butter; add milk to make dough. On floured, cloth-covered board, roll in a rectangular shape 1/4-inch thick. Spread Filling (see below) over surface of spread-out dough; roll up as for jelly roll and place in the form of a circle on a greased baking sheet. Using kitchen scissors, cut 1/2-inch slices one inch apart around the top of the roll. Spread with melted butter and sprinkle with sugar; bake in preheated 425-degree oven 30 minutes. Serve with a hot tomato sauce.

Serves 4 to 6.

Thoroughly combine all Filling ingredients.

Left: Roll up as for jelly roll. *Center:* Cut 1/2-inch slices 1 inch apart around top of roll. *Right:* Bake in 425-degree oven 30 minutes.

Smoked Venison Pizza

1 envelope granulated yeast
1¼ cups water, divided
1 tbsp butter or margarine
1 tbsp sugar
1 tsp salt
3 cups flour, divided
1 tbsp olive oil
3 tbsp Italian cheese, grated
12 slices fresh tomatoes
12 slices Monterey Jack cheese
1½ cups smoked venison, ground

Pour granulated yeast into 1/4 cup tepid water; stir once after letting it stand 5 minutes. Place butter, sugar, and salt in big bowl; add 1 cup hot water and stir until all ingredients are dissolved. Let set; when lukewarm, add yeast-water mixture. Gradually mix in half of the flour, using hand or electric beater. Add remaining flour and knead on lightly floured board to form smooth dough. Place in greased bowl; brush top with soft shortening. Cover. Let rise in warm place until double in bulk, about 45 minutes; then punch down and divide in half. Form each half into ball; place on greased baking sheet. Press out with palms of hands into a circle about 12 inches in diameter, making edges slightly thick. Brush each circle of dough lightly with olive oil and sprinkle with grated cheese. Arrange tomato and cheese slices so that each circle is divided into quarters. Heap venison on top. Bake in preheated 400-degree oven 25 minutes.

Makes 2 12-inch pizzas.

Smoked Rabbit Pie with Buttermilk Crust

3 medium potatoes, diced
4 carrots, diced
1 medium onion, sliced
1/2 pkg frozen peas
1 small can green beans, drained
1½ to 2 cups smoked rabbit, chopped
2 cans chicken gravy
Basic Seasoning or salt and pepper to taste

In water cook together the potatoes, carrots, and onion until almost done. Add peas; continue cooking. Drain all but 2 tbsp liquid from vegetables and stir in green beans, smoked rabbit, and gravy. Season to taste. Pour into baking dish and top with Buttermilk Crust (see below). Bake in 350-degree oven about 30 minutes or until brown.

Buttermilk Crust

2 cups sifted flour
1/2 tsp baking soda
3/4 tsp salt
1/3 cup shortening
3/4 cup buttermilk

Mix together dry ingredients. Cut in shortening; add buttermilk and mix well. Pat out to size of baking dish and place over smoked-rabbit mixture.

Serves 4 to 6.

Salads

Smoked Squirrel Salad

1½ cups French dressing
1/2 cup Roquefort cheese, crumbled
1/2 head iceberg lettuce
1/2 head romaine lettuce
1/2 bunch watercress
1 small head chicory
2 hard-cooked eggs, chopped
2 tomatoes, peeled, chopped
Lettuce leaves
1½ cups smoked squirrel, chopped
6 strips cooked bacon, chopped
1 hard-cooked egg white, chopped
1 hard-cooked egg yolk, sieved
2 tbsp chives, chopped
3 medium avocadoes, sliced

Combine French dressing and Roquefort cheese; chill. Chop iceberg lettuce, romaine lettuce, watercress, and chicory. Add chopped eggs and tomatoes. Line a flat serving plate with lettuce leaves. Mound chopped-green mixture in center. Top with layer of squirrel, then bacon. Make each layer slightly smaller in diameter than preceding one, so salad becomes cone-shaped. Sprinkle bacon with chopped egg white and sieved egg yolk. Sprinkle with chives. Place avocado around base of salad. Serve with cheese-dressing mixture.

Serves 8.

Chinese Garden Smoked Rabbit Salad

6 tomatoes
Salt
1/4 cup water
1/2 cup vinegar
1/4 cup sugar
Basic Seasoning or salt and pepper to taste
1½ tsp monosodium glutamate
1/4 tsp garlic, minced
2 cans (1 lb ea) bean sprouts, drained
2 tbsp red pepper, diced
2 tbsp onion, diced
1/4 cup vegetable oil
1 cup smoked rabbit, diced
1/4 cup crushed pineapple
1/4 cup mayonnaise

Peel tomatoes and scoop out centers. Sprinkle inside with salt and invert to drain thoroughly. Heat water and vinegar in saucepan. Stir in sugar, seasoning, monosodium glutamate, and garlic. Pour seasoned mixture over bean sprouts, red pepper, and onion. Stir; let cool. Add vegetable oil; toss salad lightly and cool. Drain 1 tbsp liquid from salad mixture. Combine salad mixture with rabbit and pineapple. Blend reserved liquid into mayonnaise and stir into salad. Fill tomato cavities and serve on crisp salad greens.

Serves 6.

Smoked Rabbit Chop Suey

Smoked Smelt Salad

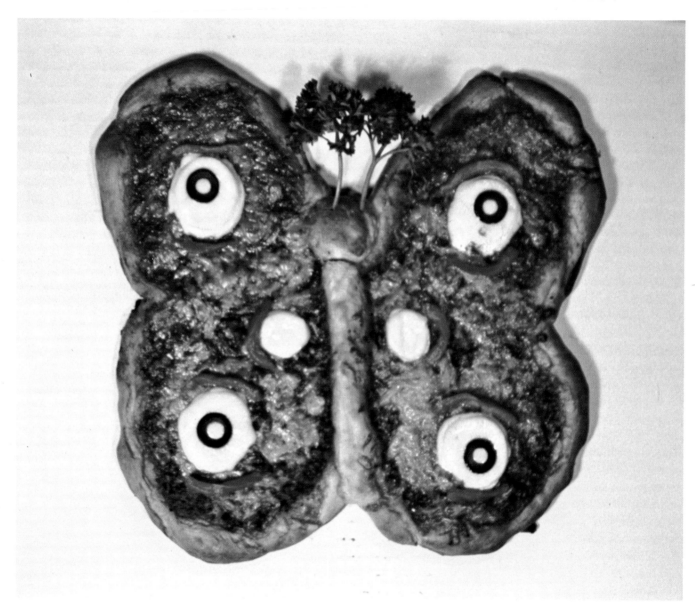

Smoked Breakfast Sausage Pizza

Smoked Venison and Vegetable Salad

2 tbsp Russian salad dressing
1/2 tsp lemon rind, grated
2 cups smoked venison, diced
1 cup celery, sliced
1 cup cooked peas, chilled
1/4 cup radishes, sliced
1 can (5 oz) water chestnuts, drained,
   sliced
Salt to taste
2/3 cup mayonnaise
1 to 2 tsp curry powder
Lettuce cups
Watercress

Combine Russian dressing and lemon rind. Pour over venison in large bowl. Add celery, peas, radishes, water chestnuts, and salt. Blend together mayonnaise and curry powder; toss with smoked venison and vegetables. Chill 15 to 20 minutes. To serve, shape lettuce into cups on salad plates; spoon smoked venison mixture into each. Garnish with watercress.

Serves 4.

Curried Rabbit in Salad Ring

2 envelopes unflavored gelatin
3⅓ cups chicken broth, divided
1 tbsp curry powder
1½ cups mayonnaise, divided
3½ tsp onion, minced, divided
1 tsp salt
Dash pepper
2 cups celery sliced, divided
1/4 cup pimiento, diced
4 hard-cooked eggs, chopped
1 tbsp lemon juice
Basic Seasoning or salt and pepper to
   taste
3 cups smoked rabbit, diced
1 cup seedless green grapes, halved
1/2 cup almonds, slivered, divided
Crisp greens

Soften gelatin in 1 cup cold chicken broth 5 minutes. Add curry powder; heat until mixture simmers and gelatin is dissolved. Remove from heat. Add remaining chicken broth, 1 cup mayonnaise, 2½ tsp onion, salt, and pepper; beat slightly until smooth. Chill until mixture begins to set. Fold in 1 cup celery, pimiento, and hard-cooked eggs. Pour into 6-cup ring mold. Chill about 3 hours or until firm. Combine 1/2 cup mayonnaise, 1 tsp onion, lemon juice, and seasoning. Add smoked rabbit, 1 cup celery, grapes, and all but 1 tbsp almonds. Mix lightly. Unmold salad ring onto serving plate. Fill center of ring with rabbit salad. Sprinkle with reserved almonds. Garnish with salad greens.

Serves 6 to 8.

Smoked Venison Suprise Salad

4 cups smoked venison, diced
1½ cups celery, sliced
3/4 cup green pepper strips
1 cup cucumber, diced
1 pink grapefruit, peeled, sectioned and
    cubed
1/3 cup French dressing
1 cup mayonnaise
1 tsp curry powder
1 tbsp onion, minced
1 tbsp parsley, chopped
Crisp greens
1 tsp chives, chopped
1 tbsp capers, drained

Combine smoked venison, celery, green pepper, cucumber, and grapefruit in large bowl. Add French dressing; chill at least 1 hour. Combine mayonnaise, curry powder, onion, and parsley. At serving time, drain French dressing from smoked venison mixture. Line large serving plate with crisp greens. Spoon venison mixture into greens; pour curry-mayonnaise dressing over salad. Sprinkle with chives and capers.

Serves 8.

Smoked Squirrel Salad Loaf

1 envelope unflavored gelatin
1⅔ cups chicken broth, divided
Salt to taste
1 tsp onion, grated
1½ tsp lemon juice
1 hard-cooked egg, sliced
6 stuffed olives, sliced
1½ cups smoked squirrel, diced
1/2 cup cooked peas
3 tbsp celery, chopped

Soften gelatin in 1/3 cup cold broth and dissolve in remaining broth, heated in top of double boiler. Add salt, onion, and lemon juice. Pour a layer of the gelatin mixture 1/4-inch deep in bottom of a greased loaf pan or mold; chill until firm. Let remaining gelatin thicken but not set. Arrange a design with the sliced egg and olives, pressing lightly into the firm gelatin in the mold. Add the squirrel, peas, and celery to the thickened gelatin-broth mixture and pour it carefully over the sliced egg and olives. Chill until firm. Unmold and slice for serving.

Serves 4 to 6.

Smoked Rabbit and Potato Salad

2 cups smoked rabbit, chopped
1/4 cup sweet pickles, chopped
1/2 cup celery, chopped
1 tbsp onion, chopped
1/2 cup cooked potatoes, diced
Basic Seasoning or salt and pepper to
    taste
1 tbsp liquid from sweet pickles
1/2 tbsp lemon juice
1/4 cup mayonnaise

Thoroughly combine smoked rabbit, sweet pickles, celery, onion, potatoes, and seasoning. Blend pickle juice, lemon juice, and mayonnaise together and mix with smoked rabbit mixture. Chill for about 1 hour to blend flavors.

Serves 4.

Sandwiches and Sandwich Fillings

Smoked Rabbit Sandwich Spread with Sweet Pickles

1 cup smoked rabbit, minced
2 tbsp onion, minced
2 tbsp green pepper, minced
1/4 cup sweet pickles, minced
1/3 cup mayonnaise
Basic Seasoning or salt and pepper to taste

Combine all ingredients and mix well. Chill. Serve between buttered slices of bread; garnish with lettuce and sweet pickles.

Makes about 2 cups.

Smoked Rabbit Sandwich Spread with Olives

2 cups smoked rabbit, minced
1/2 cup carrots, chopped
1/2 cup stuffed olives
1/2 cup salami, cubed
Basic Seasoning or salt and pepper to
    taste
1/2 cup grated cheese

Put smoked rabbit, carrots, olives, and salami through a grinder; season to taste and work into a paste with a heavy spoon. Spread on well-buttered bread; sprinkle with cheese and decorate with additional quartered olives.

Serves 8.

Smoked Venison Burgers

1 egg, beaten
1/2 cup mayonnaise
1 tbsp lemon juice
1 tbsp onion, chopped
Dash pepper
2 cups smoked venison, chopped
Fat or pure vegetable oil
6 to 7 toasted buns

Combine egg, mayonnaise, lemon juice, onion, and pepper; mix well. Stir in smoked venison. Drop venison mixture by large spoonfuls into small amount of hot fat or oil in skillet. Flatten each spoonful of venison mixture with back of spoon to form a patty. Brown patties on both sides. If desired, place a slice of American or Swiss cheese on each browned venison burger and broil until cheese melts. Serve on toasted buns.

Makes 6 to 7.

Deluxe Smoked Venison Sandwiches

2 pkgs (3 oz ea) cream cheese
1/4 cup milk
1/2 tsp parsley flakes
1/8 tsp onion powder
1 tsp dry mustard
1/4 tsp pepper
1 egg, separated
2 tsp lemon juice
1 cup smoked venison, chopped
4 club rolls, toasted
2 tbsp mayonnaise
1 tbsp Parmesan cheese, grated

Blend cream cheese, milk, parsley, onion powder, mustard, and pepper in saucepan. Cook over medium heat until mixture starts to bubble. Stir some of the hot mixture into the beaten egg yolk, blending rapidly. Return to the remaining hot mixture in saucepan; cook 1 minute longer or until mixture starts to bubble again. Remove from heat; blend in lemon juice and smoked venison. Cut thin slices from top of each roll. Hollow out rolls; spoon about 1/2 cup venison mixture into each roll. Blend mayonnaise and Parmesan cheese. Beat egg white until stiff peaks form; blend into mayonnaise mixture. Top each roll with a generous amount of egg white and mayonnaise mixture. Broil 6 inches from heat about 3 minutes or until topping is puffed and lightly browned.

Serves 4.

Delicacies

Smoked Rabbit Stew

2 cups smoked rabbit, cubed
2 cups turkey broth
1 cup tomatoes
2½ cups whole kernel corn
2½ cups lima beans
1 medium onion, chopped
1/4 tsp ginger
Basic Seasoning or salt and pepper to taste

Combine all ingredients in a 3- to 4-qt kettle. Heat to boiling. Reduce heat to simmering and continue cooking until stew is thickened, about 1 hour. Stir occasionally. Season to taste. Serve with crackers or toast.

Serves 6 to 8.

Savannah Smoked Rabbit

2 cups smoked rabbit, diced
2 tbsp butter or margarine
1 tbsp flour
1 cup water, heated
2 tbsp ham, minced
2 tbsp onion, minced
2 tbsp parsley
2 tbsp celery, chopped
Basic Seasoning or salt and pepper to taste
1/2 cup Swiss cheese, diced
1/4 cup Italian salami, minced

In heavy skillet heat smoked rabbit in butter; remove rabbit and keep warm. Blend flour with butter. Stir until smooth and add water, stirring until thickened. Add remaining ingredients, except rabbit; stir well and let cook 30 minutes. Add rabbit and cook until meat is thoroughly warm; serve immediately.

Serves 4.

Smoked Raccoon and Spaghetti

1 pkg (6 oz) uncooked spaghetti
1 tbsp salt
4 cups water
2 slices bacon, diced
3/4 cup onion, sliced
3½ cups stewed tomatoes
Basic Seasoning or salt and pepper to taste
Dash cayenne
2 cups smoked raccoon, cubed
Parmesan cheese, grated

Cook spaghetti in boiling salted water until tender. Wash in cold water and drain. Fry bacon until crisp; add onions. Cook until onions are tender and slightly brown. Add tomatoes and seasonings. Cover and simmer for 30 minutes. Add smoked raccoon and spaghetti; blend well and cook, covered, 15 minutes. Serve hot and sprinkle with Parmesan.

Serves 4.

Smoked Rabbit and Avocado Newburg

4 tbsp butter or margarine
4 tbsp flour
Salt to taste
Dash nutmeg, ground
Dash cayenne
1 egg yolk, beaten
1½ cups chicken broth
1 tbsp lemon juice
3 tbsp dry sherry
2 cups smoked rabbit, diced
1 medium avocado, peeled
Patty shells or toast points

Melt butter in medium-size saucepan. Blend in flour and seasonings; remove from heat. Combine egg yolk and broth; gradually add to flour mixture. Cook over medium heat, stirring constantly, until mixture thickens and comes to a boil. Carefully stir in lemon juice, sherry, and smoked rabbit. Just before serving, scoop out avocado with melon-ball cutter; dice remaining avocado. Add avocado to sauce; heat through. Serve in patty shells or on toast points.

Serves 4.

To prevent that unattractive dark rim from forming on a left-over portion of avocado, simply butter the cut edge.

Creole of Smoked Rabbit

2 tbsp butter or margarine
2 tbsp flour
2 tbsp ham, chopped
3 tbsp celery, chopped
2 tbsp green pepper, chopped
2 tbsp parsley, chopped
3 tbsp onion, chopped
Basic Seasoning or salt and pepper to
   taste
Paprika
2 cups consommé, heated
1 clove
Pinch mace
2 cups smoked rabbit, diced

In skillet melt butter and stir in flour. Stir in ham, celery, pepper, parsley, and onion. Season to taste; stir 2 minutes. Add consommé, clove, and mace; simmer 1 hour. Strain and stir in smoked rabbit; cook until heated thoroughly. Serve on rice, toast, or hot biscuits.

Serves 4.

Smoked Elk Florentine

1 pkg (10 oz) fresh spinach
1 can (10 oz) frozen cream of potato
  soup
3/4 cup milk
4 tbsp Parmesan cheese, grated
2 cups smoked elk, diced
2 tbsp butter or margarine, melted

Cook spinach; drain well. Combine soup and milk in top of double boiler; heat over simmering water until blended and heated through. Add cheese; stir until cheese melts. Divide spinach among 4 individual ramekins or baking dishes; top each with smoked elk. Pour sauce over meat; drizzle with melted butter. Broil about 5 minutes or until sauce bubbles. Garnish with lemon slices if desired.

Serves 4.

A very delicious meat loaf can be made from the tougher and less desirable parts of wild game (neck, shank, etc.). You may smoke-roast these either in the whole or ground, but they must be cold-smoked. Naturally, the ground meat should be smoked a lesser amount of time than anything in the round.

Chapter 4

Smoked Seafood

Casseroles and Baked Dishes

Smoked Fish Au Gratin

1/4 cup butter
1/4 cup flour
1 cup fish stock
1 cup cream
2 tbsp dry sherry
1½ cups smoked fish
1 cup cheese, grated, divided
Basic Seasoning or salt and pepper to
   taste

Melt butter in saucepan; stir in flour and cook 1 or 2 minutes. In another saucepan mix together stock and cream. Bring to boil; add to the butter-flour mixture, stirring until smooth and thickened. Add sherry, fish, and half the cheese. Season to taste. Place in a greased shallow baking dish; sprinkle with remaining cheese and bake in a preheated 350-degree oven until golden brown.

Serves 4.

Smoked Fish, Cheese, and Tomato on Bed of Potato

4 servings instant mashed potatoes
1/3 cup green onions, sliced
1/3 cup green pepper, chopped
2 cups smoked fish, flaked
1 large tomato, peeled, sliced
3 slices mozzarella cheese
1/2 tsp oregano
Basic Seasoning or salt and pepper to
   taste

Prepare instant mashed potatoes as package directs. Stir in onions and green pepper. Spoon mixture evenly into a greased oblong baking dish. Arrange smoked fish on mashed potatoes around edge of baking dish. Overlap alternating slices of tomato and cheese on potatoes down center of dish. Sprinkle oregano and seasoning over top. Bake in preheated 350-degree oven for 15 minutes or until cheese melts.

Serves 4.

Smoked Fish Soufflé

3 tbsp butter
3 tbsp flour
1 cup evaporated milk
1/2 cup water
Salt to taste
4 eggs, separated
2 cups smoked fish, flaked

Melt butter and blend in flour. Heat to scalding the milk and water; add with salt to butter-flour mixture. Cook until thickened, stirring constantly. Pour slowly over stiffly beaten egg yolks. Add smoked fish. Fold in stiffly beaten egg whites. Pour into greased 1½-qt baking dish; place in pan of hot water and bake in 350-degree oven 45 to 50 minutes.

Serves 4.

Chipper Smoked Fish Loaf with Fluffy Lemon Sauce

1/2 cup celery, chopped
1/2 cup onion, chopped
2 tbsp butter or margarine
1 can (10½ oz) cream of celery soup
3 eggs, slightly beaten
1½ cups potato chips, crushed
2 tbsp parsley
1/2 cup water
1 tbsp lemon juice
1/2 tsp marjoram
4 cups smoked fish, flaked
Fluffy Lemon Sauce (see below)

Sauté celery and onion in butter until tender. Combine with remaining ingredients, except smoked fish and lemon sauce; mix well. Fold in smoked fish. Grease 9 x 5-inch loaf pan and fill with smoked-fish mixture. Bake in 350-degree oven for 50 to 60 minutes or until firm. Let stand 10 minutes before removing from pan. Serve with Fluffy Lemon Sauce.

Serves 6 to 8.

Fluffy Lemon Sauce

2 tbsp butter or margarine
2 tbsp flour
1/2 tsp salt
1/4 tsp paprika
1¼ cups milk, scalded
1/2 cup mayonnaise
2 tsp lemon juice

In skillet melt butter; blend in flour, salt, and paprika. Add scalded milk; cook, stirring constantly, until thickened and smooth. Add mayonnaise and lemon juice; stir and heat to serving temperature.

Smoked Catfish Casserole

3 tbsp onion, chopped
3 tbsp green pepper, chopped
1 tbsp butter or margarine, melted
2 tbsp pimiento, diced
1 can (10½ oz) cream of chicken soup
1 can (10½ oz) cream of celery soup
2/3 cup milk
1 tbsp lemon juice
2 cups smoked catfish, flaked
2 cups potato chips, crushed

Sauté onion and green pepper in butter for 3 minutes or until tender; remove from heat. Combine with pimiento, soups, milk, lemon juice, and smoked catfish; mix well. Place 1 cup crushed potato chips in bottom of greased 1½-qt casserole; add smoked catfish mixture. Sprinkle remaining potato chips on top. Bake in 350-degree oven 30 minutes.

Serves 6.

Smoked Fish Biscuit Loaf

1½ cups smoked fish
1 cup cooked lima beans
1 cup American cheese, diced
1/4 cup onion, chopped
Basic Seasoning or salt and pepper to taste
1½ pkg (8 oz) refrigerated biscuits

Blend together all ingredients, except biscuits. Prepare biscuits according to package directions. Between waxed papers roll out dough into rectangle, about 12 x 14 inches. Place on ungreased baking sheet. Spread fish mixture down center of dough, covering an area about 4 inches wide. At each side of filling cut 7 strips. Starting at top, bring the first two opposite strips up over filling, overlapping slightly; pinch overlapping sections together to seal. Continue to lace opposite strips over filling, tucking last ends underneath. Bake 20 to 25 minutes in preheated 425-degree oven.

Serves 6.

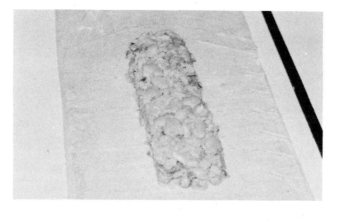

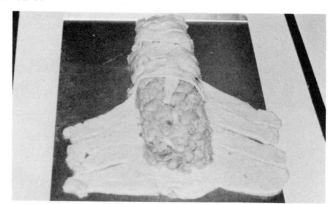

Top left: Spread fish mixture down center of dough. *Top right:* Cut dough into 7 strips on each side; lace opposite strips over filling. *Botton left:* Loaf ready for baking. *Bottom right:* The delectable finished product.

Smoked Fish and Cottage Cheese Supreme

2 cups cottage cheese, divided
2 cups cooked rice
2 cups smoked fish
1 can (10½ oz) cream of mushroom soup
Salt to taste
Dash tabasco sauce

Thoroughly mash 1 cup cottage cheese with fork. Mix well with remaining ingredients. Place in shallow 2-qt greased casserole. Top with remaining cottage cheese. If desired, sprinkle mixture with crushed corn chips and garnish with sliced stuffed olives and additional smoked fish. Bake 30 minutes in 350-degree oven.

Serves 6 to 8.

Smoked Fish Loaf Delight

1 egg
3/4 cup milk
1 cup soft bread crumbs
2 cups smoked fish, flaked
1 cup cheddar cheese, shredded
1 tsp green pepper, grated
1 tsp lemon juice
1/2 tsp celery salt
1/2 tsp garlic salt
1/2 cup fine dry bread crumbs
2 tbsp melted butter

Beat together egg and milk; add soft bread crumbs, flaked fish, cheese, green pepper, lemon juice, and seasonings. Place in a 9 x 5-inch loaf pan; top with dry bread crumbs mixed with melted butter. Bake at 350 degrees for 30 minutes. Slice and serve.

Serves 6.

Smoked Fish and Noodle Bake

1/3 cup green pepper, diced
4 tbsp butter, melted, divided
1 can (10½ oz) cream of celery soup
1 cup milk
1½ cups American cheese, shredded
2 cups smoked fish, flaked
1/2 cup cooked noodles
1/4 cup ripe olives, sliced
1 cup soft bread crumbs

In saucepan sauté green pepper in 2 tbsp butter until tender. Add soup and milk; heat until bubbly, stirring constantly. Add cheese; stir until melted. Stir in smoked fish, drained noodles, and olives. Turn into greased 2-qt casserole. Combine crumbs and remaining butter. Sprinkle over casserole mixture. Bake, uncovered, at 350 degrees for 30 to 35 minutes.

Serves 6.

Smoked Fish Casserole with Cheese Swirls

3 tbsp safflower or peanut oil
1/3 cup green pepper, chopped
1/4 cup onion, chopped
1/3 cup flour
1½ cups milk, scalded
2 cups smoked fish, flaked
1 can (10½ oz) chicken with rice soup
1 tbsp lemon juice
Cheese Swirls (see below)

In saucepan heat oil; sauté green pepper and onion for 5 minutes. Stir in flour; gradually add scalded milk. Cook over low heat, stirring constantly, until sauce is smooth and thickened. Stir in smoked fish, soup, and lemon juice. Pour into a greased 2-qt baking dish. Top with Cheese Swirls. Bake in preheated 350-degree oven for 30 minutes.

Serves 4.

Cheese Swirls

1½ cups flour
1/2 cup toasted wheat germ
2½ tsp baking powder
1/8 tsp salt
1/2 cup shortening
2/3 cup milk
2 cups sharp cheddar cheese, shredded
1/8 tsp cayenne pepper

Combine flour, wheat germ, baking powder and salt. Cut in shortening; add milk and mix with a fork until dough holds together. Turn out on lightly floured board and knead gently about 12 times. Roll out dough into a 12-inch square. Sprinkle with cheese and pepper. Roll up as for jelly roll and cut into 1/2-inch slices.

Baked Smoked Fish Puff

5 to 6 slices bread, cubed, divided
Butter or margarine
1 cup American cheese, grated, divided
1 cup smoked fish, flaked, divided
3 eggs, beaten
Salt to taste
Dash pepper
1/4 tsp paprika
1/4 tsp dry mustard
2 cups milk

Spread bread slices with butter and cut into 1-inch squares. Grease casserole and place 1/2 of the cubes in the bottom. Spread 1/3 of the cheese over cubes and 1/3 of the smoked fish over cheese. Add the rest of the bread cubes and the smoked fish and 1/3 of the cheese. Combine eggs, salt, pepper, paprika, and mustard; stir in milk. Pour liquid mixture over the bread cube mixture; top with remaining cheese. Place casserole in pan of hot water and bake in 325-degree oven for about 40 minutes or until firm and knife inserted in center comes out clean.

Serves 4.

Japanese Mandarin Smoked Fish Loaf

2 cups smoked fish, flaked
2 eggs, beaten
1/4 tsp Worcestershire sauce
2 cups fresh bread crumbs
1/2 cup milk
Salt to taste
1/4 tsp poultry seasoning

Spicy Mandarin Oranges

1/4 cup sugar
1/4 cup vinegar
Dash nutmeg
Few whole cloves
Small stick cinnamon
2 cans (11 oz) mandarin oranges

Combine all ingredients, mixing lightly but well. Turn into greased 9 x 5-inch loaf pan and bake in preheated 350-degree oven for 45 minutes or until firm in the center. Spoon hot Spicy Mandarin Oranges (see below) over and around before serving.

Serves 4.

Combine sugar, vinegar, spices, and liquid drained from oranges. Bring to a boil. Reduce heat to medium; cook and stir mixture until syrupy. Add orange segments to hot syrup. Simmer 1 or 2 minutes to heat through.

Frosted Smoked Salmon Loaf

4 cups smoked salmon, flaked
2½ cups fresh bread crumbs
2 eggs, beaten
1 egg white, slightly beaten
1 cup milk
1/3 tbsp parsley flakes
2 tbsp instant minced onion
Basic Seasoning or salt and pepper to taste
1/2 pkg (4 servings) instant mashed potatoes
1 egg yolk
Butter or margarine, melted

Line a 9 x 5 x 3-inch loaf pan lengthwise with strip of foil; make the strip long enough to extend slightly beyond the pan at both ends for ease in lifting baked loaf from pan. Grease pan and foil. Combine smoked salmon, bread crumbs, eggs, egg white, milk, parsley, onion, and seasoning in large bowl; mix thoroughly. Turn into prepared pan. Bake in 350-degree oven 45 to 50 minutes or until firm. While loaf bakes, prepare instant mashed potatoes according to package directions; beat in egg yolk. Increase oven heat to 425 degrees. Remove loaf from pan; place on cooky sheet. Spread mashed potatoes on top and sides of loaf; brush with melted butter. Bake until potatoes are tipped with brown. Serve with a dill sauce.

Serves 8.

Scalloped Smoked Fish

2 cups smoked fish, flaked
2 cups medium white sauce
2 tbsp onion, grated
Basic Seasoning or salt and pepper to
   taste
1 cup bread crumbs
2 tbsp butter

In alternate layers in a buttered baking dish, place fish, sauce, onion, and seasoning. Sprinkle top with buttered bread crumbs and bake at 350 degrees for 30 minutes.

Serves 4.

Smoked Salmon Bake

1½ cups packaged precooked rice
1½ cups water, boiling
2 cups smoked salmon, flaked
Basic Seasoning or salt and pepper to
   taste
2 tbsp instant minced onion
2 egg whites
1 egg
2 tbsp butter or margarine, melted

Add rice to boiling water; cover, remove from heat, and let stand 5 minutes. Combine rice, smoked salmon, seasoning, and onion. Beat together egg white and egg; add to salmon mixture, blending well. Press into well-buttered 9 x 5 x 3-inch loaf pan. Brush top with melted butter. Bake in 375-degree oven 30 minutes or until firm and golden. Serve with a lemon sauce.

Serves 4 to 6.

Scalloped Smoked Fish, Almonds, and Noodles

1 pkg (4 oz) small noodles, uncooked
1 tbsp butter
1 tbsp flour
Basic Seasoning or salt and pepper to
   taste
1 cup milk
1 to 2 tbsp lemon juice
1 cup smoked fish, flaked
1/3 cup almonds, toasted, crushed
Buttered bread crumbs or buttered
   cracker crumbs

Heat oven to 350 degrees. Cook noodles as directed on package. Make sauce by melting butter in saucepan. Blend in flour and seasoning. Cook over low heat until smooth and bubbly. Remove from heat; stir in milk. Return to heat and cook 10 minutes until thickened, stirring constantly. Sprinkle lemon juice over smoked fish. Add cooked noodles, toasted almonds, and white sauce; toss lightly. Turn into 8 individual shells or greased 2-qt casserole. Top each with bread crumbs. Bake 10 to 15 minutes.

Serves 6.

Smoked Fish and Noodle Casserole

1¼ cups noodles, uncooked
1 cup smoked fish, flaked
1/2 cup mayonnaise
1/3 cup onion, chopped
1 cup celery, sliced
1/4 cup green pepper, chopped
1/4 cup pimiento, chopped
Salt to taste
1 can (10½ oz) cream of celery soup
1/2 cup milk
1 cup American cheese, shredded
1/2 cup blanched almonds, slivered

Cook noodles according to package directions in boiling salted water until tender; drain. Combine noodles, smoked fish, mayonnaise, vegetables, and salt. Blend soup and milk; heat through. Add cheese; cook and stir until cheese melts. Add to noodle mixture. Turn into 2-qt casserole. Top with almonds. Bake in 350-degree oven about 30 minutes.

Serves 6 to 8.

Most cheeses may be frozen in 1-pound or smaller chunks. Thaw in refrigerator.

Smoked Shrimp Casserole

1/2 cup green pepper, chopped
1/2 cup onion, chopped
2 tbsp butter or margarine
2 cups smoked shrimp
2 cups cooked rice
1 can (10½ oz) tomato soup
3/4 cup light cream
1/4 cup dry sherry
1 tbsp lemon juice
Salt to taste
1/4 tsp nutmeg
Toasted almonds
Parsley

Sauté green pepper and onion in butter until tender but not brown. Stir in remaining ingredients, except almonds and parsley. Pour into 2-qt casserole. Bake in 350-degree oven 30 minutes or until hot. Trim with toasted almonds and parsley.

Serves 6 to 8.

Smoked Fish Cheese Loaf

2 cups smoked fish, flaked
1½ cups cheese, grated
1 egg, beaten
Few grains pepper
3 tbsp milk
1 tbsp melted butter
Salt to taste
Cracker or bread crumbs

Mix all ingredients, adding cracker or bread crumbs to make a stiff mixture. Pack into a greased loaf pan. Cover the top with buttered crumbs. Bake at 375 degrees until golden brown.

Serves 4.

Elegant Smoked Fish Loaf

1/2 cup mayonnaise
1 cup cream of celery soup
1 egg, beaten
1/2 cup onion, chopped
1/4 cup green pepper, chopped
1 tbsp lemon juice
Salt to taste
2 cups smoked fish, flaked
1 cup fine dry bread crumbs
Curly endive
Lemon wedges
Cucumber twists

Combine mayonnaise, soup, egg, onion, green pepper, lemon juice, and salt; mix well. Add smoked fish and bread crumbs; toss lightly. Place in a well-greased 9 x 5-inch loaf pan and bake at 350 degrees 1 hour. Unmold and surround with endive. Garnish with lemon wedges and cucumber twists.

Serves 4 to 6.

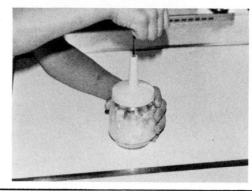

Savory Smoked Fish Loaf

2 cups smoked fish, flaked
1½ cups soft bread crumbs
3/4 cup cooked or canned tomatoes
2 tbsp melted fat
1 egg, beaten
1 tbsp onion, minced
Basic Seasoning or salt and pepper to taste

Combine all ingredients; pack into greased loaf pan. Bake at 350 degrees until firm, about 45 minutes.

Serves 4 to 6.

Smoked Fish Loaf with Sour Cream

1/3 cup sour cream
1/2 cup milk
3 eggs, separated
2 cups herb-seasoned croutons
2 cups smoked fish
3 tbsp snipped parsley, divided
1/4 cup onion, chopped fine
2 tbsp lemon juice
Basic Seasoning or salt and pepper to taste
1 cup mayonnaise
1 tbsp prepared mustard

Place sour cream, milk, and egg yolks in mixing bowl; beat well. Mix in croutons. Let stand 10 minutes or until croutons are softened. Beat until mixture is smooth. Add smoked fish, 1 tbsp parsley, onion, lemon juice, and seasoning; mix only until combined. Set aside. In mixing bowl beat egg whites until stiff but not dry. Fold 2/3 of the beaten egg whites into smoked fish mixture. Spread evenly in greased 9 x 5-inch loaf pan. Bake in preheated 375-degree oven about 30 minutes or until knife inserted in center comes out clean. While smoked fish mixture is baking, measure mayonnaise and mustard into small mixing bowl; mix well. Gently fold in remaining beaten egg whites just before spreading over smoked fish mixture. Remove casserole from oven, spread egg white mixture over top. Return to oven and continue baking about 5 minutes or until topping is firmly set and lightly browned. Remove from oven; sprinkle 2 tbsp parsley over top.

Serves 4 to 6.

Deviled Smoked Shrimp

1/4 cup plus 1 tbsp butter
1/4 cup flour
1/2 tsp paprika
1/8 tsp pepper
1/2 tsp dry mustard
1 tsp onion, grated
1½ cups milk, heated
1½ cups smoked shrimp, chopped
1 pimiento, minced
1/2 cup stuffed olives, sliced
2 tbsp dry white wine
Salt to taste
1 to 2 tbsp fine crumbs

Melt butter; blend in flour, paprika, pepper, mustard, and onion. Gradually add milk and cook, stirring, until thickened. Add remaining ingredients, except crumbs. Pour into shallow 2-qt baking dish and top with crumbs. Dot with 1 tbsp butter. Bake in 400-degree oven 15 minutes, or until crumbs are browned.

Serves 4.

Smoked Fish Mediterranean

1 can (4 oz) pimiento, drained, diced, divided
1½ cups raw rice
1 clove garlic, crushed
2 tbsp butter or margarine
1 tbsp instant minced onion
1/4 tsp dried leaf oregano
Salt to taste
2 vegetable bouillon cubes
2 cups water
1½ cups dry white wine, divided
1 cup cheddar cheese, grated
2 cups smoked fish, flaked
2 tbsp vegetable oil

Combine half the pimiento with rice, garlic, butter, onion, oregano, and salt in a greased 3-qt casserole. Combine bouillon cubes, water, and 1 cup wine in a saucepan. Heat until bouillon cubes are dissolved. Pour over rice mixture. Cover; bake in preheated 350-degree oven until rice is almost tender and liquid is absorbed, about 40 minutes. Stir in remaining wine. Combine cheese, smoked fish, vegetable oil, and remaining pimiento. Make a hollow in the center of rice mixture; fill with smoked fish mixture. Bake, uncovered, about 15 minutes longer.

Serves 6 to 8.

Easy-to-fix Smoked Fish Loaf

3 tbsp fat
3 tbsp flour
1 cup milk, scalded
Basic Seasoning or salt and pepper to taste
2 tbsp parsley, minced
2 cups smoked fish, flaked
2 cups bread crumbs
1 egg, beaten

Prepare sauce by blending together hot fat and flour in skillet. Slowly stir in scalded milk. Cook until thickened, stirring constantly. Add seasoning. Mix the sauce with remaining ingredients. Bake in loaf pan in 350-degree oven 30 minutes or until browned.

Serves 4.

Smoked Fish and Potato Puff

1/2 pkg (4 servings) instant mashed potatoes
3 eggs, separated, beaten
2 tbsp parsley, minced
2 cups smoked fish, flaked
1 tbsp onion, minced
1 tbsp lemon juice
Basic Seasoning or salt and pepper to taste

Prepare potatoes according to package directions. Stir in egg yolks, parsley, smoked fish, onion, lemon juice, and seasoning; blend well. Gently fold in stiffly beaten egg whites; turn mixture into lightly buttered 2-qt casserole. Bake in 325-degree oven about 1 hour or until puffy and golden.

Serves 4.

Smoked Catfish Soufflé

2 cans (10½ oz ea) cream of celery or
   mushroom soup, divided
1 tbsp parsley, chopped
1/4 tsp leaf thyme, crumbled
Dash pepper
4 eggs, separated, beaten
1 cup smoked catfish, flaked
Salt to taste
1/4 tsp cream of tartar
1/2 cup milk

Heat 1 cup of soup; remove from heat. Add parsley, thyme, pepper, and egg yolks; stir in smoked catfish. Beat egg whites, salt, and cream of tartar until stiff but not dry. Fold into smoked catfish mixture. Turn into greased 1½-qt casserole; place in pan of hot water. Bake in preheated 325-degree oven about 1 hour until puffy and brown. Heat remaining soup and milk for a sauce to serve with soufflé.

Serves 6.

Peppers with Smoked Fish Stuffing

6 green peppers
10 to 12 soda crackers, broken
1 cup thick white sauce
2 cups smoked fish
2 tbsp chili sauce
1/2 cup bread crumbs

Cut a slice from the stem end of each green pepper; remove seeds and veins. Cook in boiling salted water 10 minutes. Rinse in cold water; drain and arrange in baking dish, cut side up. Lightly blend remaining ingredients, except crumbs. Spoon into peppers. Top with crumbs. Cover bottom of baking dish with water. (You may use tomato sauce instead of water; it's good!) Bake at 350 degrees for 45 minutes or until peppers are tender and crumb topping is brown.

Serves 6.

Elegant Stuffed Peppers

4 large green peppers
2 cups smoked fish, flaked
1/2 cup onion, minced
2 tbsp butter
1 tsp Worcestershire sauce
Basic Seasoning or salt and pepper to
   taste
1½ cups cooked rice
1 cup tomato puree
2/3 cup buttered crumbs

Cut tops from green peppers and remove seeds. Serve whole or cut in half, lengthwise. Simmer in 2 cups boiling water 5 minutes; rinse in cold water and drain. Combine remaining ingredients, except buttered crumbs; fill peppers. Top with crumbs. Bake in 8-inch-square casserole with 1/2 cup water 25 to 30 minutes at 375 degrees.

Serves 4.

Smoked Fish Loaf with Noodles

1 pkg (8 oz) wide noodles, broken, uncooked
6 hard-cooked eggs, chopped
2 cups smoked fish, flaked
1 can (6 oz) mushrooms, sliced
1/2 cup onion, minced
1/2 cup sweet pickle relish
1/3 cup butter or margarine
1/2 cup flour
Salt to taste
Few drops tabasco sauce
2 tsp Worcestershire sauce
2 tbsp lemon juice
2 cups chicken broth, heated
2 cups milk or half and half cream, scalded
1 pkg (5 oz) potato chips, crushed

Cook noodles as directed on package; drain. Combine with eggs, smoked fish, mushrooms, onion, and sweet pickle relish. Melt butter; blend in flour, salt, tabasco, Worcestershire, and lemon juice. Add chicken broth and milk. Stir over low heat until thickened; add to smoked fish mixture. Toss with a fork. Grease a 10 x 10-inch 4-qt pan. Spoon in half the smoked fish mixture; sprinkle with potato chips. Repeat, ending with potato chips. Chill overnight or 24 hours. Bake at 375 degrees for 45 minutes.

Serves 12.

Oriental-Style Dishes

Smoked Fish Chow Mein

1 cup onion, chopped
1 cup celery, sliced
1 cup green pepper, chopped
1/4 cup salad oil
1 can (10½ oz) cream of mushroom soup
2 tsp cornstarch
3/4 cup cold water
1/4 cup soy sauce
2 cups smoked fish, flaked
1 can (3 oz) mushrooms, sliced, drained
1 can (5 oz) water chestnuts, drained
1 can (1 lb) bean sprouts, drained
4 cups chow mein noodles

Cook onion, celery, and green pepper in hot oil for 2 minutes. Add soup. Blend together the cornstarch, cold water, and soy sauce; gradually stir into soup mixture. Cook until mixture thickens, stirring constantly. Add smoked fish, mushrooms, water chestnuts, and bean sprouts. Heat thoroughly. Serve hot over chow mein noodles.

Serves 6 to 8.

Far Eastern Smoked Fish Dinner

1 can (20 oz) pineapple chunks
2/3 cup vinegar
1/2 cup brown sugar
Salt to taste
3 tbsp soy sauce
2 tbsp cornstarch
1/4 cup water
3 cups smoked fish, flaked
1 medium green pepper cut in 1-inch squares
Cooked rice

Drain syrup from pineapple into measuring cup and add water to make 1 cup; combine in skillet with vinegar, brown sugar, salt, and soy sauce; bring to boil. Blend cornstarch with cold water; add to skillet. Cook, stirring constantly, until mixture thickens; boil 1 minute. Add pineapple chunks, smoked fish, and green pepper. Cook over medium heat until green pepper is crisp-tender, about 2 minutes. Serve over rice.

Serves 6 to 8.

Smoked Fish Chop Chop

1 cup water
2 tbsp soy sauce
2 tbsp cornstarch
1 tsp sugar
Salt to taste
1/2 tbsp ginger
2 tbsp cooking oil
1 clove garlic, sliced
1 pkg (6 oz) frozen Chinese pea pods, partially thawed
1½ cups celery or Chinese cabbage
1 cup green onion, sliced
1 can (5 oz) water chestnuts, drained, sliced
2 cups smoked fish, flaked
3 cups cooked rice

Combine water, soy sauce, cornstarch, sugar, salt, and ginger; blend well. Heat oil and garlic in heavy fry pan or Chinese wok* over high heat until garlic is browned. Remove garlic and discard. Add pea pods and celery; cook and stir for 2 minutes. Add green onion and water chestnuts; cook and stir for 1 minute to heat vegetables. Add soy sauce mixture; cook and stir until sauce is thickened. Place smoked fish over vegetables. Cover pan; turn heat to low and allow smoked fish to heat, about 2 minutes. Serve over hot rice.

Serves 4 to 6.

*The wok is a round-bottomed, high-sided skillet. This all-purpose cooking utensil supplies maximum heat from a small heat source, makes food tender yet crisp in a few minutes of cooking, and seals in the flavor and juices of meat and vegetables. The wok excels in a method of cooking called stir-frying, in which all the ingredients are prepared in advance, the wok is preheated, and the ingredients, starting with the foods which take the longest to cook and ending with the quickest-cooking ones, are cooked in oil by swirling them quickly around the pan with a wooden spoon or metal spatula.

Smoked Fish Fried Rice

2 cups smoked fish, flaked
1/4 cup butter
Basic Seasoning or salt and pepper to
    taste
1/4 tsp monosodium glutamate
2 eggs, beaten
5 cups cooked rice
2 tbsp soy sauce
3 green onions, chopped
1/4 cup canned mushrooms, drained,
    sliced
1/4 cup green pepper, diced
1/4 cup water chestnuts, drained, sliced
1 cup bean sprouts, drained

Sauté smoked fish in butter; add seasonings and eggs, stirring until well mixed. Add rice and cook until golden brown. Stir in remaining ingredients; cook until heated through.

Serves 6 to 8.

Smoked Fish Sukiyaki

3/4 cup soy sauce
1 cup chicken broth or stock
2 tbsp sugar
3 tbsp oil
3 cups celery, sliced
1½ cups carrots, sliced
2 bunches scallions, sliced
1/2 lb fresh mushrooms, sliced
1 Bermuda onion, sliced
1 can (5 oz) bamboo shoots, drained
3 cups smoked fish, flaked
1 pkg (10 oz) spinach, drained
2 cans (1 lb each) bean sprouts, drained
2 tbsp butter
Cooked rice

Blend soy sauce, chicken broth, and sugar; set aside. Heat oil in large skillet; sauté celery, carrots, scallions, mushrooms, onion, and bamboo shoots for 7 minutes or until crisp-tender, stirring frequently. Stir in smoked fish and soy sauce mixture. Continue cooking for 5 minutes. Add spinach; cover and cook 3 minutes longer. Meanwhile, sauté bean sprouts in butter until golden brown. Serve with bean sprouts and hot rice.

Serves 8 to 10.

Smoked Shrimp Fried Rice

1/4 cup butter
2 cups smoked shrimp, halved
Basic Seasoning or salt and pepper to taste
1/4 tsp monosodium glutamate
2 eggs, beaten
5 cups cooked rice
3 tbsp soy sauce
3 green onions, chopped
1/4 cup canned mushrooms, sliced
1/4 cup green pepper, diced
1/4 cup water chestnuts, drained, sliced
1 cup bean sprouts, drained

Melt butter in skillet; add shrimp and seasonings. Cook until lightly browned, stirring frequently. Add eggs, stirring until well mixed with other ingredients. Add rice; cook until a golden color. Stir in remaining ingredients; cook until thoroughly heated. Serve at once.

Serves 6.

Chowders, Soups, Stews, Etc.

Where do each of the dishes in the glossary below begin and end? Basically, they are liquid dishes, so different, yet so similar. The information given here should help the reader to differentiate them.

Bisque: A thick rich soup made from meat or fish, especially shellfish.

Borsch: A Russian soup with innumerable recipes, but all including beets, sometimes cabbage, and served with sour cream.

Bouillabaisse: A fish stew or chowder much esteemed in the south of France.

Chowder: A stew, usually made of clams or fish with salt pork and vegetables.

Gumbo: A soup or stew which is thickened with the seedpods of okra.

Soup: Liquid food made by simmering meat, vegetables, etc. in water or milk; distinguished from broth, which is usually strained.

Stew: A dish made by simmering slowly and gently, usually using a preparation of meat or fish and vegetables. Two of the most widely known types of stew are Irish stew and mulligan stew. Irish stew uses the ingredients available in an area. In Ireland, mainly lamb, potatoes, turnips, onions, and carrots are used. The stew is not too highly seasoned. Mulligan stew is made of odds and ends of meat and vegetables, especially as made by hoboes; onions, carrots, chickens, etc.

Smoked Seafood Bisque

1 cup tomato juice
1/2 cup tomato puree
2 cups smoked fish
1 small clove garlic, crushed
Basic Seasoning or salt and pepper to taste
1 cup light cream
Lemon juice
Paprika
Chives, dill weed, or parsley

In large pot combine tomato juice, tomato puree, smoked fish, garlic, and seasoning. Simmer slowly for 2 minutes. Gradually stir in cream and a few drops lemon juice. Garnish with paprika and chives, dill, or parsley. Serve hot or cold.

Serves 4.

Smoked Shrimp Bisque

4 tbsp butter
1 stalk celery, chopped
2 large mushrooms, chopped
1/2 onion, chopped
1/2 carrot, chopped
Pinch marjoram
Few grains mace
Basic Seasoning or salt and pepper to taste
1 can (10 oz) chicken broth
2 tsp dry sherry
1 cup smoked shrimp, chopped
1 cup whipping cream

Combine butter, celery, mushrooms, onion, carrot, and seasonings in a large pot and sauté over low heat for 10 minutes. Add chicken broth and sherry; cook 5 minutes longer. Put through a sieve. Add the smoked shrimp; simmer 1 or 2 minutes. Adjust seasoning to taste and stir in cream. Serve immediately.

Serves 6.

Smoked Fish Bisque

4 tbsp butter
1 small onion, minced
4 tbsp flour
Basic Seasoning or salt and pepper to taste
4 cups milk, scalded
1 cup smoked fish
1/4 cup cooked peas
Whipped cream

Melt butter; add onion and sauté 5 minutes until transparent. Blend in flour and season to taste. Gradually add scalded milk, stirring constantly. Heat to boiling and cook 3 minutes. Rub fish and peas through a sieve. Add to milk mixture; reheat and serve. Dollop each serving with whipped cream.

Serves 4 to 6.

Smoked Fish Bisque, Continental Style

6 tbsp butter or margarine
1 tbsp onion, minced
5 tbsp flour
1 bay leaf
1 cup chicken broth, heated
1/2 cup dry white wine
1 tbsp tomato paste
1 cup smoked fish, flaked
1 cup cream
Toast stars for garnish

Melt butter in saucepan and sauté minced onion over low heat for 5 minutes until onion is transparent. Stir in flour; add bay leaf. Gradually stir in chicken broth and cook, stirring until sauce is smooth and thickened. Stir in white wine and cook over low heat for 10 minutes, stirring occasionally. Discard bay leaf; stir in tomato paste and smoked fish. Strain soup through a sieve or put into an electric blender, 2 cups at a time, blending until smooth. Return to saucepan. When ready to serve, add cream and reheat. Pour into soup tureen and garnish with toast stars. Serve with additional toast stars on the side.

Serves 4.

Hearty Smoked Fish Chowder

1/2 lb salt pork or bacon
1/2 cup onion, diced
4 potatoes, diced
1 bay leaf
1/2 tsp pepper
Water
4 cups milk
2½ cups smoked fish, flaked

Dice salt pork or bacon; add onion and sauté until tender. Add potatoes, bay leaf, pepper, and water to cover. Cook until potatoes are almost tender. Add milk and fish; heat to boiling and simmer 10 minutes.

Serves 6.

Smoked Octopus Chowder

6 oz salt pork or bacon
2 tbsp butter
1 large onion, diced
1 large clove garlic, minced
2 stalks celery, diced
1 carrot, diced
3 tbsp flour
2 cups chicken broth, heated
3 cups clam juice, heated
2 cups smoked octopus, diced
3 cups potatoes, diced
2 cups milk
1 cup light cream
1½ oz dry sherry
1/2 oz cognac
Basic Seasoning or salt, pepper, celery
    salt, monosodium glutamate

Remove rind, if any, from salt pork or bacon and finely chop. Heat salt pork or bacon in soup pot until fat melts. Add butter, onion, garlic, celery, and carrot; sauté over low heat until onion is transparent. Stir in flour, blending well. Add chicken broth, clam juice, and octopus. Add potatoes, milk, cream, sherry, and cognac. Bring to a boil and simmer 15 minutes. Season to taste.

Serves 8 to 10.

Fancy Smoked Fish Chowder

1 chicken bouillon cube
1 cup boiling water
3/4 cup onion, chopped
1/2 cup green pepper, chopped
1 clove garlic, chopped
1/4 cup butter or margarine
1 cup whole kernel corn, drained
Salt to taste
Dash pepper
1 can (16 oz) tomatoes
1 cup okra, sliced
1/4 tsp thyme
1 whole bay leaf
2 cups smoked fish, flaked

Dissolve bouillon cube in boiling water. Cook onion, green pepper, and garlic in butter until tender. Combine all ingredients and cook for 15 minutes or until vegetables are tender. Remove bay leaf.

Serves 6.

Smoked Shrimp Chowder

1 large onion, diced
2 cloves garlic, minced
2 tbsp butter or margarine
2 large potatoes, thinly sliced
1 cup water
1 chicken bouillon cube
1 tsp paprika
Basic Seasoning or salt and pepper to taste
4 cups milk
1⅔ cups smoked shrimp

Sauté onion and garlic in butter. Cook gently in large saucepan until onion is transparent. Add potatoes, water, bouillon, and paprika; season to taste. Cook slowly until the potatoes are tender; then add milk and reheat. Add smoked shrimp; simmer for 5 minutes. Serve with biscuits.

Serves 6 to 8.

Smoked Fish Soup

1 onion, chopped
2 tbsp butter
2 tbsp flour
4 cups milk, scalded
2 cups smoked fish
2 stalks celery, chopped
1 tsp Worcestershire sauce
Dash tabasco sauce
2 tbsp dry sherry
Basic Seasoning or salt and pepper to taste
1 cup cream

Sauté onion in butter until golden. Stir in flour and gradually add milk; simmer gently. Add smoked fish, celery, Worcestershire, tabasco, and sherry; continue to simmer. Season to taste. Add cream. Heat but do not boil.

Serves 4 to 6.

Cold Smoked Fish Soup

2 cups smoked fish, flaked
1 tomato, peeled, chopped
1 cucumber, peeled, chopped
2 cups chicken bouillon
2 cups sour cream
2 tbsp fresh dill weed or chives, chopped
Basic Seasoning or salt and pepper to taste

Thoroughly mix all ingredients and season to taste. Chill and serve, garnished with fresh dill or chives.

Serves 6.

Most stews or thick soups taste better the day after they are made.

Cream of Smoked Fish Soup

4 cups milk
1 onion, sliced
2 tbsp butter
2 tbsp flour
Basic Seasoning or salt and pepper to
   taste
1 cup smoked fish, flaked

In saucepan heat milk and onion to scalding; remove onion. In skillet melt butter; blend in flour and seasoning. Add milk gradually, stirring constantly. Add smoked fish and cook until smooth and slightly thickened. (It is best to prepare the soup in a double boiler, but it can be made over direct heat if care is taken not to scorch or boil.)

Serves 6.

Variations: Omit milk and seasoning, use 2 cans (10¾ oz ea) tomato soup and 2½ cups water. Or omit milk, butter, flour, and seasoning; add one can (10½ oz) cream of mushroom soup and 1 soup can water.

Smoked Oyster Stew

2 cups smoked oysters, sliced
2 cups milk
2 cups half and half cream
2 tbsp butter or margarine
Basic Seasoning or salt, pepper, and
   celery salt
1/8 tsp paprika
1 tsp parsley, chopped

Combine oysters, milk, cream, butter, and seasoning in saucepan over medium heat. Heat, but do not boil. Sprinkle with paprika and parsley.

Serves 4 to 6.

Smoked Fish Stew

1 onion, sliced
2 tbsp salad oil
2 celery stalks, sliced
1 can (10½ oz) cream of potato soup
1 can (4 oz) sliced mushrooms
Salt to taste
2 cups smoked fish, flaked
1 can (16 oz) tomatoes
1/4 cup dry sherry
1 tsp dried dill seed
1/4 tsp tabasco sauce

In large saucepan sauté onion in salad oil until transparent. Add remaining ingredients. Simmer, covered, 10 minutes.

Serves 4 to 6.

Creamed Dishes

Smoked Fish and Eggs

3 tbsp butter or margarine
3 tbsp flour
Salt to taste
3 cups milk, scalded
2 cups smoked fish, flaked
3 hard-cooked eggs, sliced
3 tbsp green onion, sliced
Buttered toast, biscuits, or English
    muffins
Paprika

Melt butter in saucepan. Blend in flour and salt. Add milk; cook, stirring constantly, until smooth and thickened. Fold in fish, eggs, and green onion; heat. Serve on toast; garnish with paprika.

Serves 4 to 6.

Creamed Eggs in Smoked Fish Crust

2 cups smoked fish, flaked
1 slice bread, crumbled
1 egg, beaten
1 can (10½ oz) cream of mushroom soup
1/2 cup half and half cream
1 can button mushrooms, drained
1 tsp Worcestershire sauce
6 hard-cooked eggs, sliced
Parsley

Combine smoked fish, bread crumbs, and egg. Mix well and press mixture into bottom and sides of an 8-inch pie plate. Bake the smoked fish crust in a preheated 350-degree oven for 15 minutes. Combine soup, cream, mushrooms, and Worcestershire sauce; heat in top of double boiler over simmering water. Reserve a few egg slices for garnish and add remaining eggs to hot mushroom sauce. Remove pie from oven; pour in hot creamed eggs and mushrooms. Serve garnished with remaining egg slices and parsley.

Serves 4.

Smoked Shrimp Newburg

1 cup butter or margarine
2 tbsp cornstarch
Basic Seasoning or salt and pepper to
  taste
1 tsp paprika
2 cups light cream
1/2 cup dry sherry
2 egg yolks, beaten
2 cups smoked shrimp, chopped
6 slices toast

Melt butter in saucepan; blend in cornstarch, seasoning, and paprika. Remove from heat; gradually blend in cream. Cook over medium heat, stirring constantly, until mixture comes to a boil; boil 1 minute. Reduce heat; gradually stir in sherry. Blend a little hot mixture into egg yolks; then stir yolks into remaining hot mixture in saucepan. Add smoked shrimp and heat, but do not boil. Serve over hot buttered toast.

Serves 6.

Creamed Smoked Fish

2 tbsp onion, chopped
3 tbsp butter or margarine
3 tbsp flour
Basic Seasoning or salt and pepper to taste
1½ cups milk, scalded
1/2 cup sour cream
1 cup smoked fish
3 tbsp dry sherry
2 tbsp parsley, chopped
Toasted slivered almonds (optional)
Puff-pastry shells

Sauté onion in butter until transparent. Blend in flour and seasoning. Add milk; cook and stir until mixture thickens. Stir in sour cream. Add smoked fish, sherry, and parsley; heat through. Sprinkle with toasted almonds, if desired. Serve in pastry shells or spoon over toast.

Serves 4.

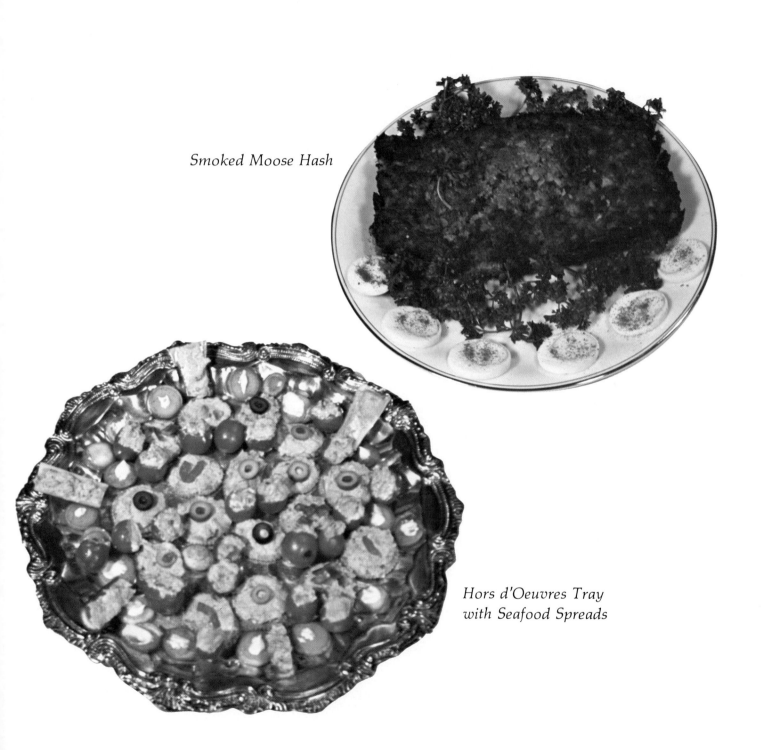

Smoked Moose Hash

Hors d'Oeuvres Tray with Seafood Spreads

*Smoked Rabbit
Macaroni Casserole*

*Cherry Tomatoes
Stuffed with
Smoked Seafood Spreads*

Smoked Salmon Pensacola

1 cup celery, sliced
1 cup fresh mushrooms, sliced
1/2 cup green onion, sliced
1/4 cup butter or margarine
1/4 cup flour
1 cup milk, scalded
1/2 cup half and half cream
1/4 cup dry sherry
2 cups smoked salmon, flaked
1/4 cup pimiento, chopped
Basic Seasoning or salt and pepper to
   taste
1 avocado
4 cups cooked rice

In saucepan sauté celery, mushrooms, and onion in butter for 8 minutes or until vegetables are tender, but not brown. Stir in flour. Gradually stir in milk and cook, stirring, until thickened. Stir in cream and sherry. Stir in salmon and pimiento; season to taste. Mix carefully and cook until heated through. Meanwhile peel, halve, and remove seed from avocado. Serve the salmon mixture over hot rice and garnish with sliced avocado.

Serves 4 to 6.

Waffles, Pancakes, and Fritters

Smoked Shrimp and Waffles

2½ cups smoked shrimp
2 hard-cooked eggs, chopped
1/2 cup celery, chopped
1/4 cup green pepper, chopped
1/2 cup mayonnaise
1/3 cup sour cream
1 tbsp wine vinegar
Basic Seasoning or salt and pepper to
   taste
1 pkg (10 oz) prebaked frozen waffles
Parsley

Set aside 6 shrimp for garnish. Cut each remaining shrimp into 3 or 4 pieces. In bowl combine shrimp, eggs, celery, and green pepper. In another bowl combine mayonnaise, sour cream, vinegar, and seasoning. Add to shrimp mixture, stirring to combine. Prepare frozen waffles in toaster or oven, according to package directions. Spread shrimp mixture on each waffle. Place in preheated 400-degree oven about 5 minutes. To serve, split reserved shrimp in half. For each serving, place 2 waffles on plate; garnish with 2 shrimp halves and sprig of parsley.

Serves 6.

Lemony Smoked Fish Crepes

Crepe Batter

3 eggs, beaten
1⅓ cup milk
3 tbsp butter or margarine, melted
1 cup sifted flour
1/2 tsp salt

Combine eggs, milk, and butter; beat well. Sift together flour and salt and gradually add to egg mixture; beat until smooth. Refrigerate at least 2 hours before making crepes. Heat a 6-inch skillet until a drop of water sizzles. Place 2 tbsp batter into greased skillet; rotate so batter covers bottom completely. When brown, turn to brown other side. To make each crepe repeat until all batter is used. Place about 2 tbsp of Filling (see below) into each crepe. Roll up and place in covered dish; heat in preheated 350-degree oven 15 minutes. Pour 1 cup Sauce (see below) over crepes before serving. Serve remaining sauce with crepes.

Makes 16.

Filling

2 cups smoked fish
3/4 cup light cream
1/2 cup parsley, chopped
1½ tsp lemon peel
1 tsp onion salt
1 tsp lemon juice

Combine all ingredients in saucepan. Heat to boiling; reduce heat and simmer 10 minutes.

Sauce

2 tbsp butter or margarine
2 tbsp flour
1/2 tsp salt
3/4 cup milk
1/2 cup light cream
1/3 cup Swiss cheese
1/3 cup Parmesan cheese
1 egg yolk, beaten

Melt butter in saucepan; blend in flour and salt. Remove from heat; stir in milk and cream until smooth. Continue cooking, stirring constantly, until thickened. Add cheeses; heat until melted. Stir 1/2 cup hot cheese mixture into egg yolk. Return to saucepan. Cook 2 minutes longer, stirring constantly.

Spinach Pancakes Stuffed with Smoked Fish

Pancake batter
1 cup cooked spinach
1/8 tsp mace
1 cup smoked fish, flaked
2 tsp butter
Tomato sauce

Prepare pancake batter according to package directions to make 12 pancakes. Add to batter coarsely chopped spinach and mace. Make pancakes and roll up each with smoked fish; dot with butter. Place them in a fireproof dish, cover, and bake in 350-degree oven 10 minutes. Serve topped with tomato sauce.

Serves 6.

Smoked Fish Fritters

1 cup flour
1½ tsp baking powder
Basic Seasoning or salt and pepper to
    taste
1/4 cup cornmeal
1 cup milk, divided
1 egg, beaten
2 cups smoked fish
1 tsp lemon juice
1 can (10½ oz) cream of asparagus soup

Sift flour, baking powder, seasoning, and cornmeal into mixing bowl. Add 3/4 cup milk and egg; beat until smooth. Sprinkle fish with lemon juice. Fold into batter. Fry tablespoonfuls of mixture in deep fat at 375 degrees for 3 to 4 minutes until golden brown. Drain on absorbent paper. Serve with sauce made by blending soup with remaining milk; heat.

Makes 16 fritters.

Egg Dishes

Scrambled Eggs with Smoked Fish

1 cup smoked fish, flaked
3 tbsp butter, divided
6 eggs
1 tbsp water
Basic Seasoning or salt and pepper to
    taste
4 slices toast
Bacon slices

Lightly sauté the smoked fish in 1 tbsp butter. Combine eggs, water, seasoning, and 2 tbsp butter cut in small pieces. Pour over smoked fish and stir slowly until cooked but still creamy. Serve over hot buttered toast. Garnish with slices of crisp bacon.

Serves 4.

Scrambled Eggs and Smoked Fish on Toast

1/4 cup green onion or chives chopped
1/4 cup butter, softened
2/3 cup Swiss cheese, shredded
6 slices toast
12 slices smoked fish
6 eggs
2 tbsp cream or milk
1½ tbsp butter
Basic Seasoning or salt and pepper to
    taste

Heat serving plates in warm oven. Combine onion, butter, and cheese; spread on toast. Top each slice with smoked fish. Keep warm in oven. Beat together eggs and cream. Melt butter in skillet and add egg-cream mixture; scramble. Season to taste. Bring plates from oven and top toast and smoked fish with scrambled eggs. Serve immediately.

Serves 4 to 6.

Peppered Smoked Fish and Eggs

3 slices bacon
3/4 green pepper, chopped
1/2 cup onion, chopped
Basic Seasoning or salt and pepper to
    taste
1½ cups smoked fish, flaked
6 eggs, beaten
1/4 cup half and half cream
1/2 tsp Worcestershire sauce

Fry bacon until crisp; drain. Crumble bacon. Cook green pepper and onion in bacon fat until tender. Add seasoning and smoked fish; heat. Combine eggs, cream, Worcestershire, and bacon. Add to smoked fish mixture and cook until eggs are firm, stirring occasionally.

Serves 6.

Smoked Shrimp and Zucchini Scramble

1 small onion, minced
1 clove garlic, minced
3 tbsp olive oil
2 cups zucchini, sliced
3 eggs
1 cup smoked shrimp, diced
Basic Seasoning or salt and pepper to
    taste

Sauté onion and garlic in olive oil until transparent, about 5 minutes. Add zucchini and cook until just tender, 3 to 5 minutes. While vegetables are cooking, beat the eggs until frothy; add smoked shrimp and seasoning. Pour the egg-shrimp mixture over the cooked vegetables, lower heat, and cook until set, lifting and turning with spatula to cook evenly.

Serves 4.

Treats Made with Rice

Risotto with Smoked Shrimp

1/4 cup olive or salad oil
1 onion, chopped
1/2 cup green pepper, chopped
1½ cups uncooked rice
1 can (6 oz) tomato paste
2½ cups chicken stock or bouillon
Basic Seasoning or salt and pepper to
   taste
1/2 tsp thyme or basil
2 cups smoked shrimp
1/2 cup cooked peas (optional)

Heat oil in heavy pan that has tight lid. Sauté onion and green pepper until golden. Add rice; cook and stir only until lightly tanned, not brown. Combine tomato paste and remaining ingredients, except shrimp and peas. Stir into rice. Cover tightly. Turn heat to lowest position; simmer without raising lid or stirring for 30 minutes. Stir in shrimp; add peas, if desired. Cover and heat 10 minutes.

Serves 4.

Smoked Fish Zarzuela

1/4 cup onion, chopped
1 small clove garlic, minced
2 tbsp butter or margarine
2 cans (10½ oz each) tomato bisque
   soup
1/4 cup half and half cream or milk
1/4 tsp tabasco sauce
Salt to taste
1 tsp brandy
1/3 cup frozen peas, thawed
1/2 cup pimiento, sliced
1/2 cup stuffed olives, sliced
2 cups smoked fish, flaked
3 cups cooked rice
Almonds, toasted, slivered

Sauté onion and garlic in butter until transparent. Stir in undiluted soup, cream, tabasco, salt, and brandy. Add peas. Cover and simmer 5 minutes. Uncover. Add pimiento, olives, and smoked fish; heat. Serve over cooked rice and garnish with almonds.

Serves 4 to 6.

Smoked Shrimp Tahiti

2 medium onions, chopped
1 clove garlic, crushed
1/4 cup butter
2 cups Coconut Milk (see below) or
　water
2 fresh tomatoes, peeled, chopped
1/2 cup celery, chopped
1 tbsp fresh coconut, shredded
1 tsp curry powder
1 tsp sugar
1 tbsp flour
Basic Seasoning or salt and pepper to
　taste
Pinch ginger
1½ cups smoked fish
4 cups cooked rice

Sauté onions and garlic in butter; add Coconut Milk, tomatoes, celery, and coconut. Bring to a boil. Blend curry powder, sugar, flour, seasoning, and ginger. Stir in a little water to make a paste and add to vegetable mixture, stirring constantly. Reduce heat, cover, and simmer about 30 minutes. Add smoked fish and continue cooking 5 minutes. Serve over hot rice.

Serves 4 to 6.

Coconut Milk

Combine in a quart saucepan a 3½-oz can or package (1⅓ cups) flaked coconut or 1 cup grated packaged type and 1⅓ cups milk. Simmer, stirring occasionally, until mixture foams up. Then strain through a very fine strainer or a double cheese cloth.

Smoked Fish Risotto with Celery

1 cup onion, chopped
1 cup celery, chopped
1/4 cup olive oil
1 can (6 oz) tomato paste
2 cups water
1 pkg (1½ oz) spaghetti sauce mix
Basic Seasoning or salt and pepper to
　taste
1 cup uncooked rice
2 cups smoked fish, flaked

Sauté onion and celery in olive oil in large skillet about 10 minutes. Add tomato paste, water, spaghetti sauce mix, and seasoning. Stir thoroughly. Cover and simmer 25 minutes. Meanwhile, cook rice in salted water, then drain. Add rice and smoked fish to spaghetti sauce mixture. Cover and heat thoroughly for about 10 minutes.

Serves 6 to 8.

Smoked Fish Risotto with Green Pepper

1 medium onion, chopped
1/2 cup green pepper, chopped
1/4 cup olive oil
1½ cups raw rice
1 can (6 oz) tomato paste
2½ cups chicken stock or bouillon
Basic Seasoning or salt and pepper to
    taste
1/2 tsp thyme or basil
2 cups smoked fish, chopped
1/2 cup cooked peas

Sauté onion and green pepper in hot olive oil in pan with tight-fitting lid until golden brown. Add rice; cook and stir only until lightly tanned but not brown. Mix in tomato paste and remaining ingredients, except smoked fish and peas. Cover tightly; simmer, without raising lid or stirring, for 30 minutes. Stir in smoked fish and peas. Cover and heat 10 minutes.

Serves 4 to 6.

Curried Smoked Fish

1 medium onion, chopped
1 clove garlic, diced
2 tbsp butter
Basic Seasoning or salt and pepper to
    taste
1/2 cup consommé
1/8 tsp cayenne pepper
2 tbsp curry powder
1 cup smoked fish, flaked
1/2 cup plain yogurt
3 to 4 cups cooked rice

Sauté onion and garlic in butter. Add remaining ingredients, except yogurt and rice; cover and simmer 7 minutes. Remove cover and continue cooking until sauce is reduced by half. Slowly stir in yogurt; heat well, stirring constantly. Serve over hot rice.

Serves 4 to 6.

Smoked Fish Pilaf

4 slices bacon, quartered
1 medium onion, chopped
2 cups canned tomatoes
1 cup uncooked rice
2 cups smoked fish, flaked
Basic Seasoning or salt and pepper to
    taste

Cook bacon until crisp; remove and reserve. Sauté onion in bacon fat. Add tomatoes; simmer 5 minutes. Transfer mixture to top of double boiler; add rice and steam, covered, 30 minutes or until rice is cooked. Add bacon and smoked fish; season to taste and place in greased baking dish. Bake in 350-degree oven about 15 minutes or until firm.

Serves 4.

Croquettes

Smoked Fish Croquettes

2 cups smoked fish
2 tbsp butter or margarine
3 tbsp flour
Salt to taste
1 tsp instant minced onion
1 cup milk, scalded
1 tbsp lemon juice
2 tsp Worcestershire sauce
1 egg, separated
1½ cups soft bread crumbs
1 cup packaged bread crumbs
1 tbsp water
Fat or pure vegetable oil
1 jar (8 oz) cheese spread, heated

Finely chop smoked fish. Melt butter in saucepan; blend in flour, salt, and onion. Gradually add milk; cook over medium heat, stirring constantly, until sauce thickens and comes to boiling. Add lemon juice and Worcestershire. Stir a small amount into slightly beaten egg yolk; stir into mixture in saucepan. Add smoked fish and soft bread crumbs, blending well. Chill several hours. Shape into 8 croquettes or patties; lightly dust with packaged bread crumbs. Combine slightly beaten egg white and water in shallow dish. Dip croquettes in mixture. Roll in remaining bread crumbs; let dry a few minutes. Pour fat or oil into skillet to a depth of 1 to 1½ inches. Heat to 375 degrees. Fry croquettes until brown; drain on paper towels. Arrange on platter; serve with heated cheese spread.

Serves 4.

Smoked Salmon Croquettes

2 tbsp butter or margarine
2 tbsp flour
Basic Seasoning or salt and pepper to taste
1 cup milk, scalded
1 cup soft bread crumbs
2 cups smoked salmon, flaked
Flour
1 egg, beaten
1½ cups bread crumbs
Fat or pure vegetable oil
1 can (10½ oz) cream of mushroom soup
1 tbsp lemon juice
1 cup light cream
1/2 tsp curry powder

Melt butter in saucepan over medium heat; stir in flour and seasoning. Add milk slowly; cook over medium heat, stirring constantly, until thickened. Remove from heat. Blend in bread crumbs and smoked salmon; chill several hours. Shape mixture into 8 croquettes or patties. Roll each lightly in flour. Dip in beaten egg; roll in bread crumbs. Pour fat or oil into skillet to a depth of 1 to 1½ inches; heat to 375 degrees. Fry croquettes until golden, turning once; drain on paper towels and keep warm. Combine soup, lemon juice, cream, and curry powder. Heat until bubbly; serve with croquettes.

Serves 8.

Fish Cakes and Patties

Smoked Fish Cakes

1/2 cup onion, chopped
2 tbsp melted fat or oil
2 cups smoked fish, flaked
1/4 cup parsley, chopped
Dash pepper
2 cups cold mashed potatoes
1 egg, beaten
1/2 cup dry bread crumbs

Sauté onion in fat until tender. Combine all ingredients, except crumbs. Shape into cakes and coat with crumbs. Fry in hot fat at medium heat 3 to 4 minutes; turn and repeat.

Serves 6.

Smoked Fish Patties

2 cups smoked fish, flaked
1 small onion, diced
1/2 cup green pepper, diced
Basic Seasoning or salt and pepper to taste
1 cup cracker crumbs
1 egg
1/2 tsp sage
Flour
2 tbsp butter or oil

Thoroughly mix all ingredients, except flour and butter. Mixture will be slightly moist. If mixture doesn't hold together, add another egg. Form patties and dip in flour. In skillet fry in butter over medium heat until golden brown on each side.

Serves 4.

Lemony Smoked Fish Patties

1 cup smoked fish, flaked
Basic Seasoning or salt and pepper to taste
1 tsp lemon juice
8 soda crackers, crushed
2 eggs, beaten
1/4 cup milk
2 tbsp parsley, chopped
2 tbsp butter or oil
Lemon wedges and parsley, for garnish

Combine all ingredients, except butter and garnishes. Shape into patties. In skillet fry in butter over medium heat until golden brown on both sides. Garnish with lemon wedges and parsley.

Serves 4.

Salads

Smoked Fish Fruit Salad

1/4 cup mayonnaise
1 can (6 oz) evaporated milk
Dash angostura bitters
2 cups smoked fish, flaked
1 tbsp lemon juice
2 oranges, peeled, chunked
1 red apple, diced
1 banana, sliced
1 cup celery, diced
1/4 cup blanched almonds, slivered
Paprika

Thin mayonnaise with canned milk; add bitters. Sprinkle fish with lemon juice; add remaining ingredients and toss with mayonnaise mixture. Serve at once in lettuce cups. Sprinkle with paprika.

Serves 6.

Avocado Filled with Smoked Fish

2 avocados
1 tbsp lemon juice
Salt to taste
1 cup celery, diced
1 cup smoked fish, flaked
1/2 cup mayonnaise
Cranberries or mandarin oranges

Cut avocados lengthwise into halves; remove seeds and sprinkle with lemon juice and salt. Combine celery and smoked fish with mayonnaise to moisten; fill centers of avocados. Garnish with cranberries or mandarin oranges.

Serves 4.

Smoked Fish Fruit Salad with Avocado-Orange Garnish

1 avocado, thinly sliced
1 tbsp lemon juice
2 cups orange (about 3 oranges),
   sectioned
2 cups smoked fish, flaked
1½ cups celery, sliced
1/2 cup blanched almonds, toasted,
   slivered
1/3 cup mayonnaise
Salad greens

Sprinkle avocado slices with lemon juice. Reserve 6 avocado slices and 6 orange sections for garnish. Cut remaining avocado slices and orange in 1-inch pieces. Combine with remaining ingredients, except salad greens; chill. Shape into a mound on salad greens and garnish with avocado and orange slices.

Serves 6 to 8.

Smoked Fish Salad in Grapefruit Half-Shell

2 medium-size grapefruit
1 cup smoked fish
3/4 cup celery, diced
1/3 cup green pepper, diced
Basic Seasoning or salt and pepper to
    taste
Lettuce leaves
Cherry tomatoes
Smoked whole shrimp (8)
Grapefruit Salad Dressing (see below)

Grapefruit Salad Dressing

1/4 cup fresh grapefruit juice
2 tbsp orange juice
1½ tsp lemon juice
1/4 tsp powdered mustard
1/2 tsp warm water
1½ tsp salad oil
Basic Seasoning or salt, pepper, and
    paprika to taste

Cut grapefruit in half crosswise and remove seeds. With sharp knife cut out sections and remove pulp. Reserve shells. Cut grapefruit sections into pieces and combine with smoked fish, celery, green pepper, and seasoning. Toss lightly. Line grapefruit shells with lettuce leaves. Fill with grapefruit mixture. Garnish with cherry tomatoes and whole shrimp. Serve with chilled Grapefruit Salad Dressing.

Serves 4.

Combine juices in small bowl. Dissolve mustard in water; let stand for 10 minutes, allowing flavor to develop. Add to juice mixture with remaining ingredients. Whip with wire whisk to blend well. Chill.

Curried Grape and Smoked Shrimp Salad

2 cups smoked shrimp, chopped
2 cups fresh seedless green grapes,
    halved
2 cups cashew nuts
1/2 cup sour cream
1/2 cup mayonnaise
2 tbsp onion, minced
2 tbsp green pepper, minced
1/8 tsp ginger
1½ tsp curry powder
Salt to taste
1 tbsp lemon juice

Place shrimp and grapes in large bowl with cashews. Blend sour cream and mayonnaise with remaining ingredients; pour over smoked shrimp and grapes, mixing well. Chill several hours. Serve with salad greens and grape clusters.

Serves 5 to 7.

Smoked Shrimp and Cabbage Salad

2 cups cabbage, sliced
1 cup carrots, shredded
3/4 cup smoked shrimp, chopped
1/2 cup Sweet and Sour Dressing
   (see below)
1 small Bermuda onion, cut in rings

Combine cabbage, carrots, and smoked shrimp. Pour Sweet and Sour Dressing over mixture. Toss thoroughly. Garnish with onion rings.

Serves 4 to 6.

Sweet and Sour Dressing

1/2 cup water
1 pkg creamy French dressing mix
3 tbsp vinegar
1/2 cup olive oil
2 tbsp sour cream
2 tbsp celery, chopped
2 tbsp chives, chopped

Pour water into mixing bowl; add dressing mix and whip until well blended. Add vinegar, olive oil, sour cream, celery, and chives. Mix thoroughly.

Makes 1⅔ cups.

Smoked Fish Mold Parisienne

2 tsp flour
1 tsp sugar
1 tsp prepared mustard
Basic Seasoning or salt and pepper to
   taste
3 egg yolks, beaten
1½ tbsp butter, melted
3/4 cup cold milk
1/4 cup vinegar
1 tbsp unflavored gelatin
2 tbsp water
2 cups smoked fish, flaked
1 cup celery, diced
2 tbsp chives, minced
1/2 cup canned peas, drained
Watercress
Mayonnaise
Paprika

In top of double boiler combine flour, sugar, mustard, and seasoning; add egg yolks, melted butter, milk, and vinegar. Place over low heat and cook, stirring constantly, until mixture is thickened. Remove from heat. Add gelatin softened in water and blend well. Heat, stirring to dissolve gelatin; cool. When mixture begins to set, add smoked fish, celery, chives, and peas. Fill a large mold; chill until firm. To serve, unmold on a bed of watercress; top with mayonnaise and dust with paprika.

Serves 6 to 8.

Smoked Fish Macaroni Salad

8 oz elbow macaroni
1 small onion, chopped
1/4 cup parsley, chopped
1 cucumber, sliced
2 cups smoked fish, flaked
1/2 tsp dry mustard
Basic Seasoning or salt and pepper to taste
6 tbsp salad oil
2 tbsp vinegar
Salad greens

Cook macaroni according to package directions. Drain and rinse with cold water. Combine macaroni with remaining ingredients, except salad greens. Line large bowl with crisp salad greens and pour salad into center.

Serves 6.

Smoked Fish Salad Loaf

1 refrigerated pkg (8 oz) avocado dip
1/4 cup sour cream
2 tsp lemon juice
1/2 tsp salt
2 cups smoked fish, flaked
1 cup cheddar cheese, shredded
1/2 cup celery, chopped
2 hard-cooked eggs
3 tbsp green onion, sliced
1 loaf Vienna or French bread
Melted butter
Leaf lettuce
Capers

In a bowl blend together avocado dip, sour cream, lemon juice, and salt. Stir in smoked fish, cheese, celery, eggs, and onion. Chill. Cut top off bread; hollow out center, leaving about 1/2-inch shell. Brush with melted butter. Line shell with lettuce and spoon in smoked fish mixture. Garnish with capers.

Serves 8.

Smoked Shrimp Salad with Tomato Wedges

1 tomato, peeled
Lettuce leaves
6 smoked shrimp
1 tbsp mayonnaise

Partially cut a tomato into 6 sections. Place on lettuce on a salad plate. Spread the tomato sections slightly apart and place a smoked shrimp between each section. Top with mayonnaise.

Serves 1.

Pickled Smoked Fish Salad Bowl

1/4 bunch curly endive
1 small head lettuce
1 cup pickled smoked fish, flaked
1/2 mild white onion, sliced and
    separated in rings
Olive oil

Tear endive and lettuce in bite-size pieces. Place pickled fish atop greens in salad bowl; place onion rings over fish. Toss at table with olive oil.

Serves 4.

Smoked Fish Salad with Roquefort

1 large head lettuce
2 cups smoked fish, flaked
Basic Seasoning or salt and pepper to
    taste
2 oz Roquefort cheese
1/2 cup cream
1 tsp brandy
1 tbsp vinegar
Pinch cayenne pepper
Orange, lemon, and tomato slices

Line salad bowl with the best of the outer leaves of lettuce head. Tear the rest and mix with smoked fish; season and pile into salad bowl. Mash cheese with fork and mix with cream, brandy, vinegar, and cayenne pepper. Sprinkle over salad and garnish with orange, lemon, and tomato slices.

Serves 4 to 6.

Smoked Fish and Tomato Mold

2 envelopes unflavored gelatin
2½ cups water, divided
2 cups tomato sauce
2 tsp sugar
Salt to taste
Dash cayenne pepper
1/4 tsp oregano
2 cups smoked fish, flaked
2 pkgs (3 oz each) cream cheese
Juice and grated rind of 1 lemon
1 small onion, minced
2 tbsp sour cream

Soften gelatin in 1/2 cup cold water; add 2 cups boiling water and stir to dissolve gelatin. Add tomato sauce, sugar, salt, pepper, and oregano. Rinse 1½-qt ring mold in cold water. Pour mixture into mold and chill until partially set. Mix smoked fish into gelatin mold and chill until firm. Mash cream cheese with fork; blend in lemon, onion, and sour cream. Cover and chill. To serve, remove gelatin ring from mold and top with sour cream mixture.

Serves 8 to 10.

Smoked Fish Salad with Eggs

3 hard-cooked eggs
Basic Seasoning or salt and pepper to
   taste
1/2 tsp prepared mustard
1/2 cup vinegar
3 large dill pickles
2 cups smoked fish, flaked
Lettuce leaves

Mash egg yolks; add seasonings. Heat vinegar to boiling and pour over egg yolks. Chop egg whites and pickles and mix with smoked fish. Combine mixtures and chill. Serve in lettuce cups.

Serves 6 to 8.

Smoked Fish Chef's Salad

1 cup smoked fish, flaked
1 cucumber, peeled, diced
1 large tomato, peeled, chopped
3 tbsp French dressing
1 tsp lemon juice
3 tbsp sour cream
1 tbsp fresh dill, chopped, or 1 tsp
   dried dill

Combine smoked fish with cucumber and tomato. Mix the French dressing with lemon juice, sour cream, and dill; blend with smoked fish mixture.

Serves 4.

Smoked Fish Mousse

1 envelope unflavored gelatin
3/4 cup water
1/4 cup vinegar
1 tbsp mustard
Salt to taste
1 small onion, chopped
2 cups smoked fish, flaked
1/2 cup celery, chopped
Few sprigs parsley
1/2 cup whipping cream, whipped to
   make 1 cup

Soften gelatin in water. Heat to dissolve; cool. Blend with vinegar, mustard, salt, and onion. Mix well; add smoked fish, celery, and parsley. Blend until smooth. Combine with whipped cream and pour into mold. Chill several hours until thickened.

Serves 6.

Crunchy Smoked Fish Salad

1 pkg (3½ oz) potato chips
2 cups smoked fish, flaked
1/4 cup sweet cucumber relish
3/4 cup celery, diced
1 tbsp onion, grated
1/2 cup mayonnaise
Basic Seasoning or salt and pepper to taste
1 tbsp lemon juice
1/4 cup light cream

Crush potato chips and set aside. Combine smoked fish, relish, celery, and onion. Blend mayonnaise, seasoning, lemon juice, and cream; mix with fish-relish mixture and chill. When ready to serve, mix in lightly the crushed potato chips. Mound in lettuce cups. Serve at once.

Serves 4 to 6.

Smoked Fish Salad with Remoulade

3 hard-cooked eggs
1/2 tsp mustard
1 tsp anchovy paste
1 cup mayonnaise
1/3 cup red table wine
1/4 tsp onion powder
2 cups smoked fish, flaked
1 cup celery, diced
2 tbsp parsley
Lettuce

Mash egg yolks to a paste with mustard and anchovy paste. Blend in mayonnaise, wine, and onion powder. Add smoked fish, celery, and parsley. Chill. To serve, heap in lettuce cups; sprinkle sieved hard-cooked egg whites over top.

Serves 4 to 6.

Smoked Fish Louis

Shredded lettuce
2 cups smoked fish, flaked
1 cup celery, diced
2/3 cup mayonnaise
1/3 cup chili sauce
3 tbsp dry sherry
3 tbsp ripe olives, chopped
Tomato wedges
2 hard-cooked eggs, sliced

Line chilled salad plates with lettuce. Mix smoked fish and celery; mound on lettuce. Cover with dressing made by mixing mayonnaise, chili sauce, sherry, and olives. Garnish with tomato wedges and egg slices.

Serves 6 to 8.

Jellied Smoked Fish Mold

1 cucumber
1 cup stuffed olives, chopped
1 envelope unflavored gelatin
1½ cups water, divided
1/3 cup lemon juice
Salt to taste
3/4 cup mayonnaise
1½ cups smoked fish, flaked
1 cup celery, diced
1/4 cup green pepper, diced
1/2 tbsp onion, minced

Pare cucumber and slice in-half lengthwise. Scoop out center and fill with olives. Place halves together; set aside. Soften gelatin in 1/2 cup water. Heat to dissolve; cool. Add lemon juice, 1 cup water, and salt. Chill until mixture begins to thicken. Gradually beat in mayonnaise. Pour layer of gelatin mixture into greased 9 x 5-inch loaf pan or mold; chill. When firm, arrange a layer of smoked fish, celery, green pepper, and onion on top, then place stuffed cucumber in center. Carefully alternate layers of the gelatin and smoked fish mixtures until cucumber is covered. Chill until firm. Serve on crisp lettuce; garnish with parsley, lemon sections, cucumber slices, and radish roses.

Serves 6.

Smoked Fish and Cucumber Mousse

1 envelope unflavored gelatin
1/4 cup cold water
1 bouillon cube
1/2 cup boiling water
1/2 cup mayonnaise
1 tsp Worcestershire sauce
1 tbsp onion, minced
1 tbsp vinegar
Basic Seasoning or salt and pepper to taste
2 cups smoked fish, flaked
1½ cucumbers, diced
1/2 cup cream, whipped to make 1 cup
Lettuce leaves

Soften gelatin in cold water. Dissolve bouillon cube in boiling water. Add to gelatin and stir until gelatin dissolves; cool. Add mayonnaise, Worcestershire, onion, vinegar, and seasoning to taste; blend well. Chill until thick. Beat with rotary egg beater until light and foamy. Fold in smoked fish, cucumber, and whipped cream. Turn into 1-qt mold; chill until firm. Serve with additional mayonnaise on lettuce leaves. (This mousse looks handsome molded in a fish-shape mold.)

Serves 4 to 6.

Pickled Smoked Fish and Egg Salad

1 cup pickled smoked fish, flaked
3 hard-cooked eggs, sliced
1 cup celery, diced
Basic Seasoning or salt and pepper to taste
2 tbsp parsley, minced
1/4 to 1/3 cup mayonnaise
2 tbsp onion, minced
2 tbsp lemon juice
Lemon wedges

Combine pickled fish, eggs, and celery. Blend remaining ingredients, except lemon wedges; stir into fish mixture. Serve on crisp greens and garnish with lemon wedges.

Serves 4.

One-Dish Smoked Fish Salad

1 cup mayonnaise
1 tsp prepared mustard
1/2 tsp dried tarragon
Salt to taste
1 tbsp lemon juice
2 cups cooked potatoes, sliced
2 cups celery, diced
2/3 cup radishes, sliced
1/3 cup green onions, sliced with tops
2 cups smoked fish, flaked
Lettuce leaves

Combine mayonnaise, mustard, tarragon, salt, and lemon juice. Fold in potatoes; cover and refrigerate several hours to blend flavors. Fold in celery, radishes, onions, and half the smoked fish. Mix carefully. Arrange in center of lettuce-lined serving bowl and garnish with remaining smoked fish. Serve with additional mayonnaise thinned with lemon juice or cream.

Serves 6 to 8.

Smoked Fish Waldorf Salad

2 cups smoked fish, flaked
1 cup apples, diced
1/2 cup celery, chopped
1/4 cup nutmeats, chopped
1/2 cup mayonnaise
Lettuce

Combine all ingredients, except lettuce; serve over lettuce.

Serves 6.

Smoked Salmon Mousse with Horseradish

2 envelopes unflavored gelatin
1¾ cups water
1 cup mayonnaise
2 tbsp lemon juice
2 tsp prepared horseradish
1/2 tsp paprika
2 cups smoked salmon, flaked
1/2 cup celery, diced
1/4 cup pimiento-stuffed olives, chopped
1 tbsp onion, chopped
1/2 cup whipping cream, whipped to
　make 1 cup

In saucepan soften gelatin in water. Stir over low heat until gelatin is dissolved; cool slightly. Blend together mayonnaise, lemon juice, horseradish, and paprika; gradually stir in cooled gelatin mixture. Chill until partially set. Fold in salmon, celery, olives, and onion. Whip cream until soft peaks begin to form; fold into salad. Turn into 5½-cup mold. Chill until firm. Trim with lettuce, if desired.

Serves 5.

Smoked Salmon Mold

1/4 cup sugar
2 envelopes unflavored gelatin
2 cups water, divided
Salt to taste
1/4 cup vinegar
4 tsp lemon juice, divided
1 cup cucumber, peeled, diced
1/2 cup celery, diced
1/2 cup mayonnaise
2 cups smoked salmon, flaked
Lettuce leaves

In saucepan combine sugar, 1 envelope gelatin softened in 1/4 cup water; and salt; stir in 1 cup water, vinegar, and 3 tsp lemon juice. Cook and stir until mixture boils and gelatin is dissolved. Remove from heat; chill until partially set. Fold in cucumber and celery; turn into 5-cup mold. Chill until almost set. Soften 1 envelope gelatin in 1/4 cup water; heat and stir to dissolve. Combine mayonnaise, 1/2 cup water, and 1 tsp lemon juice. Stir in salmon; blend in dissolved gelatin and spoon over cucumber layer. Chill until firm. Unmold and serve on lettuce leaves.

Serves 6.

Smoked Salmon and Cucumber Mold

Top layer

1 envelope unflavored gelatin
1 cup milk, divided
1 cup cucumber, chopped
1 tbsp prepared horseradish
Salt to taste

Soften gelatin in 1/2 cup milk. Heat in top of double boiler until dissolved. Stir in remaining milk, cucumber, horseradish, and salt. Pour into 9 x 5-inch loaf pan; chill until thickened.

Bottom Layer

1/4 cup lemon juice
1 cup water, divided
1 envelope unflavored gelatin
1 can (3 oz) mushrooms
1 tbsp vegetable oil
Salt to taste
1/4 tsp dill weed, dried
1 cup smoked salmon, flaked
2 hard-cooked eggs, chopped
1 tbsp onion, grated

Combine lemon juice and 1/4 cup water. Add gelatin to soften; then heat until dissolved. Drain mushrooms, reserving liquid. Combine vegetable oil with mushroom broth and remaining water to make 1 cup. Add dissolved gelatin, salt, and dill weed; mix well. Add smoked salmon, eggs, mushrooms, and onion. Mix gently; pour onto partially set top layer. Chill until firm or overnight.

Serves 4.

Smoked Fish Garden Salad

3 cups smoked fish, flaked
French dressing to moisten
1 cucumber, peeled, cubed
1 tbsp onion, chopped
Basic Seasoning or salt and pepper to
   taste
1/2 cup mayonnaise
Lettuce
1 pimiento, chopped
Capers

Moisten the smoked fish with French dressing and chill thoroughly. Mix the smoked fish, cucumber, onion, and seasoning with sufficient mayonnaise to bind together ingredients. (The mayonnaise may be thinned with a little cream or canned milk.) Serve on crisp lettuce leaves on a large platter. Garnish with pimiento and capers.

Serves 6 to 8.

Molded Smoked Fish Waldorf Salad

2 pkgs (3 oz each) lime gelatin
3¾ cups water, divided
1 unpeeled apple, sliced
1 cup unpeeled apple, chopped
1/2 cup celery, diced
1/2 cup pecans, broken
2 cups smoked fish, flaked
1 cup mayonnaise
2 tbsp lemon juice
2 tbsp milk
Lettuce leaves

Dissolve gelatin in 1¾ cups boiling water. Stir in 2 cups cold water; chill until partially set. Spoon part of the mixture into a 5½-cup ring mold. Arrange unpeeled apple slices in gelatin around bottom; chill. Fold chopped apple, celery, and pecans into remaining gelatin. Hold at room temperature until gelatin in mold is almost set; then carefully spoon over top of first layer. Chill until firm. Unmold gelatin onto lettuce-lined plate. Fill center of ring with chilled smoked fish. Blend together mayonnaise, lemon juice, and milk. Pour a small amount of dressing over smoked fish and serve with remaining dressing.

Serves 6 to 8.

Smoked Shrimp Salad Supreme

1 large avocado
1 tbsp lemon juice
1/2 cup sour cream
1 tbsp chili sauce
1/2 tsp lemon peel, grated
2 tsp minced onion
Salt to taste
2 cups smoked shrimp, chopped
1 cup celery, sliced
1/2 cup green pepper, diced
1/4 cup slivered almonds
Salad greens

Use a ball cutter or a 1/2 tsp measure to make balls from halves of the avocado. Sprinkle with lemon juice. Mix sour cream, chili sauce, lemon peel, onion, and salt; lightly toss with shrimp, celery, and green pepper. Fold in the avocado balls and slivered almonds. Serve on crisp salad greens.

Serves 6 to 8.

Seafood Soufflé Salad

1 pkg (3 oz) lemon gelatin
Salt to taste
1½ cups water, divided
1 tbsp lemon juice
1/2 cup mayonnaise
1 cup avocado, peeled, diced
3/4 cup smoked fish, flaked
1/4 cup celery, diced
1 tbsp onion, chopped

Dissolve gelatin and salt in 1 cup boiling water. Stir in 1/2 cup cold water and lemon juice. Gradually beat gelatin mixture and mayonnaise until smooth; chill until partially set. Beat until fluffy; fold in avocado, smoked fish, celery, and onion. Chill again until mixture mounds when spooned. Turn into 4-cup mold; chill until firm.

Serves 4 to 6.

Smoked Fish Luncheon Molds

1 envelope unflavored gelatin
2/3 cup cold water
1 cup sour cream
1/4 cup chili sauce
Salt to taste
1/3 cup lemonade
1 cup celery, diced
1/4 cup green pepper, diced
1 cup smoked fish, flaked
Lettuce leaves

Soften gelatin in cold water. Heat in top of double boiler, stirring until gelatin dissolves. Beat in sour cream until smooth; add chili sauce and salt to taste. Stir in lemonade. Chill until partially set; fold in remaining ingredients. Pour into 5 to 6 individual molds or 3½-cup mold. Chill until firm. Unmold and serve on lettuce leaves.

Serves 5 to 6.

Smoked Fish Salad with Lemon, Red Pepper, and Honey

4 lemons
2 cups smoked fish, flaked
1 red pepper, diced
3 tbsp olive oil
1 tbsp honey
Basic Seasoning or salt and pepper to
    taste
6 to 8 slivered almonds

Blanch the lemons in heavily salted boiling water for 3 minutes; drain and cut in thin slices. Combine smoked fish, lemon slices, and red pepper in salad bowl. Beat together oil, honey, and seasoning in a small bowl; pour over the salad. Cool for 2 hours before serving. Garnish with slivered almonds.

Serves 4 to 6.

Smoked Shrimp Salad Vinaigrette

1 cup Vinaigrette Dressing (see below)
2 cups smoked shrimp, chopped
Lettuce leaves

Vinaigrette Dressing

3/4 cup olive oil
1/4 cup vinegar
Basic Seasoning or salt and pepper to
    taste
3 tbsp dill pickle, grated
1 tsp sugar
1/8 tsp paprika
1 tsp onion, minced
1 tbsp parsley, minced
1 hard-cooked egg, grated

Pour Vinaigrette Dressing over smoked shrimp in salad bowl. Serve on lettuce leaves.

Serves 6.

Combine all ingredients, blending well (1/2 tsp curry powder may be added, if desired). Chill before serving.

Makes 2 cups.

Scandinavian Smoked Fish Salad

1/3 cup mayonnaise
2/3 cup sour cream
1 tbsp prepared mustard
1 tsp sugar
1/3 cup onion, chopped
2 cups smoked fish, flaked
1 cup dill pickles, diced
1 pkg (10 oz) frozen peas, cooked,
    cooled
1 can (16 oz) sliced red beets, drained,
    quartered
Basic Seasoning or salt and pepper to
    taste

In large mixing bowl mix together mayonnaise, sour cream, mustard, and sugar. Add remaining ingredients and toss lightly. Cover; chill several hours.

Serves 6 to 8.

Smoked Fish and Egg Salad

2 cups smoked fish, flaked
3 hard-cooked eggs, sliced
1 cup celery, diced
2 tbsp onion, minced
2 tbsp parsley, minced
2 tbsp lemon juice
Basic Seasoning or salt and pepper to
   taste
1/4 to 1/3 cup mayonnaise
Salad greens
Lemon wedges

Combine smoked fish, eggs, and celery. Blend remaining ingredients, except greens and lemon wedges; stir into smoked fish mixture. Serve on crisp greens and garnish with lemon wedges.

Serves 4.

Smoked Shrimp and Vegetable Salad

2 cups smoked shrimp
1 pkg (10 oz) frozen asparagus, cooked,
   diced
1 can (4 oz) peas, drained
1 cucumber, peeled, diced
2 cups potatoes, cooked, diced, chilled
1 large apple, peeled, diced
2 stalks celery, diced
Salt to taste
1/2 tsp sugar
3/4 cup mayonnaise
Lettuce, shredded

Combine smoked shrimp with asparagus, peas, cucumber, potatoes, apple, and celery. Season with salt and sugar. Blend with mayonnaise. Serve over lettuce.

Serves 8.

Smoked Fish Salad with Pecans

4 cups smoked fish, flaked
1 cup celery, chopped
3 hard-cooked eggs, chopped
4 sweet pickles, chopped
1/2 cup pecans, chopped
2 cups mayonnaise
Basic Seasoning or salt and pepper to
   taste

Blend fish and chopped ingredients with mayonnaise; season to taste. Chill. Garnish with additional sweet pickle slices.

Serves 10.

Smoked Shrimp Salad

2 cups smoked shrimp, chopped
Juice of 1/2 lemon
1 cup celery, diced
1 cup watercress or lettuce, chopped
3 tbsp mayonnaise
1 tbsp cream
1/4 tsp curry powder

Sprinkle smoked shrimp with lemon juice and chill. Mix shrimp with celery and watercress or lettuce. Combine mayonnaise, cream, and curry powder; moisten salad mixture with this dressing.

Serves 4.

Smoked Salmon Salad

2 cups smoked salmon, flaked
1 cup cucumber, diced
1 cup celery, diced
1 tsp onion, minced
1 tsp parsley, minced
Basic Seasoning or salt and pepper to
  taste
2 tsp lemon juice
1 cup mayonnaise
Salad greens

Combine the smoked salmon, cucumber, celery, onion, and parsley. Add seasoning and lemon juice to mayonnaise; fold gently into salmon mixture. Serve on greens.

Serves 6 to 8.

Molded Smoked Fish Salad

1 envelope unflavored gelatin
1/2 cup water
2 cups smoked fish, flaked
1/2 cup celery, diced
1 cup mayonnaise
1/4 cup sweet pickle, chopped
2 tbsp onion, chopped
2 tbsp lemon juice
1 tbsp Worcestershire sauce
Salt to taste
1 pkg (3 oz) lemon gelatin

Soften gelatin in 1/2 cup water and dissolve according to package directions. Stir into smoked fish; then add remaining ingredients, except lemon gelatin. Dissolve lemon gelatin as package directs; pour half into large mold and let set until firm. Add smoked fish mixture and top with remaining lemon gelatin.

Serves 6.

Smoked Salmon Mousse with Mustard

1 envelope unflavored gelatin
1 tbsp sugar
Salt to taste
1 tsp dry mustard
1/4 cup cold water
1/4 cup vinegar
2 cups smoked salmon, flaked
1 cup celery, diced
1 tbsp capers
1/2 cup cream, whipped to make 1 cup
Lettuce leaves

Mix together gelatin, sugar, salt, and mustard in top of double boiler. Add cold water and vinegar to soften gelatin; place over boiling water and stir until gelatin is thoroughly dissolved; chill. Stir in smoked salmon, celery, and capers; fold in whipped cream. Turn into a 6-cup mold; chill until firm. Unmold on lettuce leaves and serve with salad dressing.

Serves 4.

Smoked Shrimp in Tomato Jelly

2 cans (10¾ oz each) tomato soup
2 envelopes unflavored gelatin
1 cup water, divided
1 cup smoked shrimp
1 cup stuffed olives, sliced
1/2 cup dill pickle, sliced
1/2 cup hard-cooked eggs, sliced

Heat tomato soup to the boiling point. Soften gelatin in 1/2 cup cold water; add 1/2 cup boiling water, stirring until gelatin is completely dissolved. Combine with tomato soup. Arrange first layer by alternating smoked shrimp with stuffed olives in a large mold or individual molds which have been dipped in cold water. Slowly pour in a little of the slightly cooled gelatin mixture. Let set. Make 2 additional layers, one by alternating smoked shrimp with dill pickle; the other by alternating shrimp with eggs. Pour remaining gelatin over mixture. Chill until firm. Unmold on a platter covered with watercress and garnish with more egg slices, dill pickles, or olives.

Serves 10.

Smoked Fish Fiesta Mold

2 pkgs (3 oz each) lime gelatin
3 cups water, divided
2 tbsp lemon juice
2 tsp prepared horseradish
Few drops tabasco sauce
2 cups smoked fish, flaked
2 medium oranges, peeled, chopped
    (about 1 cup)
Lettuce leaves
Mayonnaise or salad dressing

Dissolve gelatin in 2 cups boiling water. Stir in 1 cup cold water, lemon juice, horseradish, and tabasco. Chill until partially set. Fold in smoked fish and chopped oranges. Turn into 5-cup mold. Chill until firm. Unmold on lettuce leaves and serve with mayonnaise or salad dressing.

Serves 5 to 7.

Molded Smoked Fish and Potato Salad

1 pkg (3 oz) lemon gelatin
1¼ cups boiling water
2 tbsp vinegar
1/2 cup mayonnaise
2 tsp lemon juice
Salt to taste
1/4 tsp dried dill weed
2 cups smoked fish, flaked
1 cup potatoes, cooked, peeled, diced
1/2 cup cucumber, diced

Dissolve gelatin in boiling water; stir in vinegar. Chill until partially set; beat until soft peaks form. In bowl blend mayonnaise, lemon juice, salt, and dill weed. Add smoked fish and potatoes; toss lightly. Fold with cucumber into gelatin mixture. Chill until mixture mounds from a spoon. Spoon into a 8 x 8 x 2-inch pan. Chill until firm. Cut into serving portions.

Serves 6.

Smoked Fish and Potato Salad

4 cups smoked fish, flaked
2 cups cooked potatoes, peeled, sliced
4 tomatoes, peeled, sliced
1 medium onion, sliced
2 tbsp parsley, minced
1/2 cup French dressing
1 tbsp chives, minced
1 tbsp capers

Arrange alternate layers of smoked fish, potatoes, tomatoes, onion slices, and 1 tbsp parsley in a salad bowl, spooning 1 or 2 tbsp dressing on each layer. Top with remaining parsley, chives, capers and dressing. Let stand at least 1 hour in refrigerator before serving.

Serves 8 to 10.

Smoked Fish and Chili Mold

1 envelope unflavored gelatin
1¼ cups water, divided
1½ tbsp sugar
Basic Seasoning or salt and pepper to
    taste
1/4 cup lemon juice
1/4 cup chili sauce
1 cup smoked fish, flaked
2 tbsp pickle relish
Lettuce leaves

Soften gelatin in 1/4 cup cold water. Mix with sugar and seasoning; dissolve in 1 cup hot water. Add lemon juice and chili sauce; chill slightly. Fold in smoked fish and pickle relish; turn into a 3-cup mold. Chill until firm. Unmold on lettuce leaves.

Serves 6.

Smoked Salmon and Cucumber Mousse

1 cup water
1 envelope unflavored gelatin
3 tbsp lemon juice
2 cups smoked salmon, flaked
1 tsp prepared mustard
2/3 cup mayonnaise
Dash cayenne pepper
1/2 cup celery, diced
3/4 cup cucumber, diced

Heat water to simmering. Soften gelatin in lemon juice; add to hot liquid and stir until gelatin is thoroughly dissolved. Cool until mixture is slightly thickened. Stir together smoked salmon, mustard, mayonnaise, and pepper. Add thickened gelatin and blend well. Fold in celery and cucumber. Turn mixture into a 6-cup mold and chill for several hours until firm. When ready to serve, unmold on bed of crisp salad greens and garnish with cucumber slices and sprigs of mint or parsley.

Serves 4 to 6.

Smoked Smelt Salad

1 cup smoked smelt, boned, flaked
2 cups celery, minced
1 green pepper, minced
1 onion, minced
Basic Seasoning or salt and pepper to
    taste
1/2 tsp paprika
1/2 cup French dressing
1 head lettuce, shredded
2 hard-cooked eggs, sliced

Combine smoked fish and vegetables. Add seasonings; toss together with dressing and serve on shredded lettuce. Garnish with hard-cooked eggs.

Serves 6.

Variation: Use 1 cup chopped tart apple for half the celery, and omit green pepper.

Smoked Shrimp in Cucumber Ring

1 pkg (3 oz) lime gelatin
1 cup boiling water
2 tbsp lime juice
1 can (13½ oz) crushed pineapple
3/4 cup cucumber, unpeeled, shredded
2 tbsp green onion, sliced
1 cup salad oil
1/2 cup vinegar
Basic Seasoning or salt and pepper to taste
1/2 tsp dried dill weed
2 cups smoked shrimp
Lettuce leaves

Dissolve gelatin in boiling water; stir in lime juice. Chill until partially set. Combine undrained pineapple, cucumber, and green onion; fold into gelatin. Turn into 4½-cup ring mold. Chill until firm. Combine oil, vinegar, seasoning, and dill weed. Pour over smoked shrimp in a shallow dish. Cover; chill at least 24 hours, spooning marinade over smoked shrimp occasionally. Drain smoked shrimp. Unmold salad on lettuce-lined plate and fill center with the chilled smoked shrimp.

Serves 4 to 6.

Sandwiches and Sandwich Fillings

Pineapple and Smoked Fish Sandwich

1 cup smoked fish, flaked
1 tbsp mayonnaise
1 can (9 oz) crushed pineapple, well drained
16 slices bread
Melted butter
Lettuce leaves (optional)

Moisten smoked fish with mayonnaise, adding more if needed; stir in crushed pineapple. Spread between bread slices. Brush with melted butter and sauté or grill until well browned. Add lettuce leaves before serving, if desired.

Makes 8 sandwiches.

Smoked Fish Burgers

1/2 cup onion, chopped
1/4 cup melted fat or oil
1/2 cup chicken bouillon
1 cup dry bread crumbs, divided
2 eggs, beaten
1/4 cup parsley, chopped
1 tsp powdered mustard
2 cups smoked fish, flaked
Basic Seasoning or salt and pepper to
    taste
1/3 cup mayonnaise
1 tbsp sweet pickle, chopped
6 buttered hamburger rolls

Sauté onion in fat until tender. Combine in a mixing bowl with bouillon, 1/2 cup crumbs, eggs, parsley, mustard, and smoked fish; mix well and season to taste. Shape into 6 patties. Roll in remaining crumbs. In skillet fry in hot fat until brown, turning carefully to cook on both sides. Drain on absorbent paper. Combine mayonnaise and pickle. Place burgers on bottom half of each roll; dollop with about 1 tbsp mayonnaise mixture and top each with other half of roll.

Serves 6.

A stick of softened butter will spread about 25 slices of bread. A pint of mayonnaise will spread about 50 slices of bread.

Smoked Shrimp Omelet Sandwiches

8 slices bread, toasted
1/3 cup butter or margarine
8 eggs, beaten
2 tsp soy sauce
Basic Seasoning or salt and pepper to
    taste
1 tbsp chives or green onion, minced
3/4 cup green pepper, minced
1 can (8¾ oz) pineapple tidbits, well
    drained
1 medium tomato, chopped
1½ cups smoked shrimp, chopped
4 slices baked ham

Spread toast with butter. Halve 4 slices diagonally. Arrange 1 whole slice with 2 halves on opposite sides for each sandwich. Combine eggs, soy sauce, and seasoning. Melt 1/3 cup butter in large heavy skillet. Add chives and green pepper; cook 2 or 3 minutes. Pour in egg mixture. When set around edges, lift with spatula to allow uncooked egg to run under. When bottom is fairly firm, add pineapple, tomato, and shrimp. Fold without turning over and cook 5 minutes, or until mixture is cooked through. Arrange ham on toast; top each slice with a serving of omelet.

Serves 4.

Smoked Fish Sandwich

1/4 cup mayonnaise
1 tbsp onion, chopped
1 tbsp parsley, chopped
1 tsp lemon juice
8 slices pumpernickel or dark bread
Sliced smoked fish (for 4 sandwiches)

Blend together mayonnaise, onion, parsley, and lemon juice. Spread on bread; place smoked fish slices on 4 slices of bread and top with remaining slices.

Makes 4 sandwiches.

Open-Face Broiled Smoked Fish Sandwich

2 cups smoked fish, flaked
1/4 cup green onion or cucumber, minced
1/4 cup celery, minced
1/4 cup stuffed olives, sliced
1/3 cup mayonnaise
1 can (10½ oz) cream of mushroom soup
1/2 cup dry sherry
1/4 lb Swiss or American cheese, cubed
6 slices bread
Paprika

Combine smoked fish, green onion, celery, olives, and mayonnaise. Dilute soup with sherry in top of double boiler; add cheese. Cook over hot water, stirring occasionally, until cheese melts; stir well until smooth. Toast bread; arrange on baking pan. Heap smoked fish salad on each slice and pour cheese sauce over. Broil until cheese is bubbly and brown. Dust with paprika and serve immediately.

Makes 6 sandwiches.

Smoked Fish Chippers

1 cup smoked fish, flaked
1/4 cup celery, chopped
1/4 cup mayonnaise
1 tsp prepared horseradish
1 tsp prepared mustard
1 tsp lemon juice
Dash pepper
8 slices bread
1/2 cup milk
2 eggs, beaten
1¼ cups potato chips, crushed

Combine smoked fish, celery, mayonnaise, horseradish, mustard, lemon juice, and pepper. Spread smoked fish mixture on 4 slices bread. Top with remaining bread. Combine milk and eggs in shallow dish. Dip each sandwich in egg mixture, then in crushed potato chips. Pat to secure chips to bread, turning to coat each side. Brown on medium-hot, lightly greased griddle until crisp, about 4 or 5 minutes on each side.

Makes 4 sandwiches.

Smoked Fish Salad Club Sandwich

2 cups smoked fish, flaked
1/2 cup celery, chopped
1/2 cup tartar sauce
Salt to taste
18 slices bread, toasted, buttered
Lettuce
12 tomato slices

Combine smoked fish, celery, tartar sauce, and salt to taste. Chill. Spread about 1/3 cup smoked fish mixture on each of 6 slices toast; top with second slice of toast. Cover with lettuce and 2 tomato slices and third slice of toast. Secure with wooden picks and cut into quarters.

Makes 6 sandwiches.

Smoked Fish and Egg Spread

1 cup smoked fish, flaked
2 hard-cooked eggs, chopped
1/4 cup mayonnaise
1 tbsp parsley or chives, chopped
12 slices bread
Lettuce leaves

Combine smoked fish, eggs, mayonnaise, and parsley; blend well. Spread on buttered slices of bread covered with lettuce leaves.

Makes 6 sandwiches.

Smoked Fish Salad Sandwich

1 cup smoked fish, flaked
1/2 cup cucumber, diced
Lettuce leaves
2 tbsp mayonnaise
1 tbsp mustard
12 slices bread

Combine smoked fish, cucumber, half of the lettuce, shredded, mayonnaise, and mustard; blend well. Spread on buttered slices of bread with remaining lettuce.

Makes 6 sandwiches.

One cup of sandwich filling will usually make about 4 to 6 sandwiches.

Hors d'Oeuvres
with Seafood Spread,
Edged with Smoked Eggs

Smoked Shrimp Salad
with Tomato Wedges

Molded Salad with Smoked Fish

Smoked Fish (Shrimp) and Cheese, Dressed Up for Christmas

Antipasto Plate of Pickled and Smoked Items

Smoked Shrimp and Waffles

Smoked Rabbit Oriental

Card Party Tray
of Seafood Spreads

Smoked Fish and Potato Burgers

2 cups smoked fish
2 medium raw potatoes, grated
2 eggs, beaten
1 medium onion, minced
Basic Seasoning or salt and pepper to
    taste
4 hamburger rolls

Mix all ingredients into a soft batter. Fry in medium-hot skillet, allowing sufficient time for potato to cook.

Serves 4.

Smoked Shrimp Salad Sandwich

1 pkg (3 oz) cream cheese
2 tsp milk
1 tsp prepared mustard
1 cup smoked shrimp, chopped
1/4 cup celery, chopped
8 slices white bread, buttered
Lettuce leaves

Blend together cream cheese, milk, and mustard until smooth. Add smoked shrimp and celery to cream cheese mixture; mix well. Spread filling on 4 slices bread. Top with lettuce and remaining 4 slices bread.

Serves 4.

Smoked Fish and Cheddar Sandwich

2 cups smoked fish, flaked
1 cup cheddar cheese, shredded
1/3 cup green pepper, diced
2 tbsp pimiento, chopped
1/2 cup mayonnaise
1/2 tsp onion salt
12 slices bread, buttered
Lettuce leaves

Combine smoked fish, cheese, green pepper, pimiento, mayonnaise, and onion salt. Spread smoked fish filling on 6 slices bread. Top with lettuce and remaining bread.

Serves 6.

Special Treats

Smoked Fish Pasties

Pastry

1 pkg (22 oz) piecrust mix
1/3 cup sharp cheddar cheese, grated
1/3 cup wheat germ
5 to 6 tsp cold water
Milk

Filling

2 cups smoked fish
1/2 cup carrots, shredded
2 tbsp milk
1 tsp instant minced onion
1/2 cup mayonnaise
2 hard-cooked eggs, chopped
2 tbsp lemon juice
1/4 tsp pepper

Combine piecrust mix, cheese, and wheat germ. Add water, a little at a time, mixing lightly with fork. Shape dough into firm ball. Divide in half. Roll each half into a 12-inch square. Cut each into 4 squares. Combine all Filling ingredients (see opposite) in bowl; mix lightly. Spread about 1/3 cup Filling diagonally on half of each pastry square to within 1/2 inch of edges. Moisten edges with water. Fold dough over fillings to form triangles. Seal edges by pressing with floured fork. Place on ungreased baking sheet. Brush tops with milk. Prick 2 or 3 times with fork. Bake at 425 degrees for 12 to 14 minutes. Serve hot with a cheese sauce or creamed vegetable.

Makes 8.

Smoked Fish Hash

6 slices bacon
2 cups smoked fish, flaked
4 cups raw potatoes, diced
2 tbsp onion, chopped
2 tbsp parsley, chopped
Dash pepper
1/3 cup fat
1/2 cup water, heated
Dash paprika

Fry bacon until crisp in 10-inch fry pan. Drain; crumble bacon. Combine bacon, smoked fish, potatoes, onion, parsley, and pepper. Place mixture in hot fat in fry pan; pour water over top. Cover; cook over medium heat 7 minutes. Turn mixture and cook, uncovered, 6 minutes longer until lightly browned. Stir occasionally to mix in browned potatoes. Sprinkle with paprika.

Serves 6.

Refrigerated or cold onions will not cause any tears.

Smoked Fish Clemenceau

1/4 cup butter or margarine
1 cup diced frozen French-fried potatoes
Dash garlic powder
1½ cups smoked fish
1 pkg (10 oz) frozen green peas, cooked
1 can (3 oz) mushrooms, sliced
Parsley, chopped

In large skillet melt butter; add potatoes and garlic powder. Cook over medium heat until potatoes are golden brown. Add smoked fish, peas, and mushrooms, including mushroom liquid. Heat mixture, stirring occasionally, until liquid is absorbed, and fish and vegetables are hot. Garnish with parsley.

Serves 4.

Smoked Fish Boat Dinner

1 loaf (10- to 12-inch) French bread,
    unsliced
2 tbsp butter or margarine, melted
2 cups smoked fish
1 cup cooked peas
1 cup celery, diced
1/4 cup pimiento, chopped
1/2 cup mayonnaise
Basic Seasoning or salt and pepper to
    taste
3 fresh tomatoes
2 tbsp French dressing
Dried basil leaves, crushed
6 slices sharp American cheese, halved
    diagonally

Halve bread lengthwise. With fork remove 1/2 cup crumbs from each half. Reserve crumbs. Brush inside surface of bread with melted butter. Combine smoked fish, peas, celery, pimiento, and reserved crumbs. Toss lightly with mayonnaise and seasoning. Spoon evenly into each "boat." Place on rack of broiler pan. Halve tomatoes. Brush with French dressing; sprinkle with seasoning and basil leaves. Place on broiler rack with smoked fish boats. Broil 6 inches from heat, about 3 minutes. Top boats with cheese slices. Return to broiler until cheese bubbles and melts, about 2 minutes. Serve immediately.

Serves 6.

Smoked Fish Nuggets

2 cups smoked fish, flaked
1 tbsp celery, minced
1½ tsp Worcestershire sauce
1 egg, beaten
Basic Seasoning or salt and pepper to
taste
1/2 cup mashed potatoes
1 tbsp onion, grated
1 tbsp butter
1/4 lb sharp cheese, cubed
1 cup dry bread crumbs

Combine all ingredients, except cheese and bread crumbs; mix thoroughly. Form walnut-size balls and insert cube of cheese into each nugget. Roll in bread crumbs. Fry in deep fat at 375 degrees about 4 minutes or until golden brown. Serve with egg sauce, if desired. (These may be frozen for 3 to 4 weeks.)

Serves 4.

Like a browned piecrust? Sprinkle a little sugar on top and it will brown lightly.

If you have several onions to peel, cover with hot water a few minutes. This will allow the skins to slip off easily.

Dill, sold in various ways—dill salt, dill seed, fresh dill, dried dill, etc.—is an excellent flavoring for all fish dishes.

To obtain some onion juice, sprinkle the cut surface of an onion with salt; then scrape with a knife or spoon.

To test the temperature of a griddle, sprinkle a few drops of water on it. If the drops sit and simmer, it is hot enough for egg dishes. If the drops dance off the griddle, it is ready for steaks or griddle cakes, pancakes, and flapjacks.

Serve all egg dishes on or in glass, china, or stainless-steel flatware. The sulfur in eggs will discolor silver.

If you get a liquid dish too salty, add slices of raw potato and cook until potato is parboiled. Remove with slotted spoon.

Chapter 5

Sausage

Casseroles and Baked Dishes

Smoked Sausage Oven Pancake

2 eggs
1½ cups milk
1½ cups flour
1 tsp baking powder
1 tsp salt
1/2 lb smoked link sausage, summer
    sausage, or salami, thinly sliced
1 small onion, thinly sliced
1 cup sharp cheddar cheese, shredded

Beat eggs; add milk, flour, baking powder, and salt. Mix until blended. Butter two 8- or 9-inch round cake pans very well. Arrange slices of sausage and onion in the pans and pour pancake batter over them, dividing it evenly between the two pans. Sprinkle cheese evenly over the batter. Bake in 400-degree oven for about 20 minutes or until golden brown. Serve hot.

Serves 6 to 8.

Top left: Slice sausage and onion. *Top right:* Arrange slices of sausage and onion in pans and cover with pancake batter. *Bottom left:* Sprinkle cheese over batter. *Bottom right:* Bake and enjoy the delectable result.

Smoked Sausage, Apple, and Yam Casserole

1 cup applesauce
Lemon juice (if sauce is canned)
2 cups cooked yams, mashed
1 tbsp butter, melted
1/2 tsp salt
1/2 tsp cinnamon
1/2 tsp ground cloves
Grating of nutmeg
2 eggs
1 lb smoked sausage links
3 tbsp brown sugar

Mix applesauce with lemon juice. Add to yams, butter, and seasonings; stir in eggs. Put in greased casserole; arrange smoked sausage links on top in spoke design. Sprinkle with brown sugar; cover and bake in 375-degree oven 30 to 40 minutes, or until set.

Serves 4 to 6.

Smoked Sausage Lasagne

1 tbsp butter or margarine
3/4 lb ground beef
1/2 cup onion, chopped
1 clove garlic, minced
1 can (1 lb 12 oz) tomatoes
1 can (6 oz) tomato paste
1½ tsp basil
1½ tsp oregano
Salt to taste
1 tsp sugar
1 lb smoked sausage links
1 pkg (8 oz) lasagne noodles, cooked, drained
1 cup cottage cheese
12 oz mozzarella cheese, sliced
1/2 cup Parmesan cheese, grated

Melt butter in skillet; stirring often, add beef, onion, and garlic and cook until meat is crumbly. Add tomatoes, tomato paste, basil, oregano, salt, and sugar; mix well. Cover and simmer about 1 hour, stirring occasionally. Thinly slice 1/2 of the sausage links; chop remaining links. Add chopped sausage to sauce 15 minutes before end of cooking time. Spoon 1/3 of meat sauce over bottom of shallow 3-qt casserole, about 2½ inches deep. Top with a layer of lasagne noodles, cottage cheese, mozzarella cheese, meat sauce, and Parmesan cheese, using 1/2 of each ingredient; repeat process. Top with sliced sausage. Bake in preheated 350-degree oven until hot and bubbly, about 40 minutes. Let cool 15 minutes before serving.

Serves 6 to 8.

Smoked Sausage-Apple-Noodle Casserole

1 lb smoked sausage links
3 cups noodles, cooked
1 cup sweetened applesauce
2 tsp lemon juice
1/8 tsp nutmeg
1/2 cup cheddar cheese, grated

Prick sausages well with a sharp-tined fork and lay them in a pan; bake in 400-degree oven 20 minutes. Drain on paper toweling. Stir 2 tbsp drippings into noodles and arrange half of them in greased medium casserole. Combine applesauce, lemon juice, and nutmeg; pour on top of noodles. Add rest of noodles and lay sausage on top. Sprinkle with cheese and bake in 350-degree oven 20 minutes, uncovered.

Serves 4 to 5.

Top-of-the-Stove Dishes

Glazed Smoked Sausage

1 lb smoked breakfast sausage
1/2 cup flour
1 pat butter
Juice of 1 orange
4 oz sherry
1 tbsp berry jelly
1/2 tsp sugar
1/8 tsp cinnamon
1/8 tsp mace

Remove sausage meat from casing; form into 4 patties. Poach in water for about 10 minutes; roll in flour and put into frying pan with butter to brown. Meanwhile, combine orange juice, sherry, jelly, sugar, cinnamon, and mace; add to sausage. Simmer until thickened and patties are glazed. When serving, pour remaining sauce over meat.

Serves 4.

Smoked Sausage Chowder

1/2 lb smoked link sausage
2 tbsp butter or margarine
1/3 cup onion, chopped
1 cup celery, chopped
1 cup milk
1/4 cup flour
1 cup beef bouillon, heated
1/4 tsp pepper
1 cup cooked potatoes, cubed
1 cup cooked lima beans

In large saucepan or Dutch oven brown sausage links; remove and chop into bite-size pieces. Add butter to saucepan and sauté onion and celery until soft. Meanwhile, mix flour with milk to make a smooth mixture. Add bouillon, milk-flour mixture, sausage, and remaining ingredients to saucepan; mix well. Simmer 10 to 15 minutes, stirring occasionally. Serve piping hot and garnish with chopped parsley if desired.

Serves 6 to 8.

Smoked Sausage with Sauerkraut

2 cups onion, chopped
2 cups unpeeled apple, chopped
2 tbsp butter or margarine
1 can (1 lb 11 oz) sauerkraut, drained
1 cup water
1/4 cup brown sugar, firmly packed
1 tbsp caraway seeds
6 whole cloves
1 bay leaf
1 lb smoked sausage, chopped
1 cup sour cream

In skillet or Dutch oven sauté onion and apple in butter until tender, not brown. Add sauerkraut, water, brown sugar, caraway seeds, whole cloves, and bay leaf; mix well. Cover; simmer about 1 hour to blend flavors. About 15 minutes before end of cooking time, add sausage to sauerkraut mixture. Remove bay leaf. Dollop each serving with sour cream.

Serves 6.

Smoked Sausage Toast

3/4 lb smoked breakfast sausage
2 tsp parsley, chopped
1/3 cup American cheese, grated
1 tbsp prepared mustard
10 slices hot buttered toast

Remove sausage meat from casing and chop as it cooks in hot skillet; brown until done. Drain off all fat. Put sausage into mixing bowl and add remaining ingredients, except toast, mixing thoroughly. Spread on toast.

Makes 10.

Pastry Delights

Smoked Salami and Cheese Raisin Bread

1 cake compressed yeast or 1 envelope
   dry yeast
1 cup lukewarm water
1½ tbsp sugar
Salt to taste
3 cups sifted all-purpose flour
1½ cups smoked salami or smoked ham,
   diced
1½ cups cheddar cheese or Swiss
   cheese, diced
1 cup seedless raisins

Stir yeast into warm water with sugar and salt. Beat in flour, a little at a time. Knead on floured board until dough is soft and springy, about 5 minutes. Cover with waxed paper and let rise in a warm place until double in bulk. With your fingers gently knead in remaining ingredients until evenly distributed throughout dough. Shape into 2 loaves and put into heavily-greased loaf pans. Cover and let rise until double. Bake in a 350-degree oven 50 minutes or until crusty and browned on top. For sandwiches, slice thin and spread with butter, mayonnaise, and lettuce.

Makes 2 loaves.

Smoked Breakfast Sausage Pizza

Crust

1½ cups pancake mix
1/4 cup cooking oil
2/3 cup milk

Put pancake mix in bowl; stir in oil with fork. Add milk, mixing lightly. Form a 12-inch circle on greased cooky sheet; bake in 450-degree oven 10 minutes.

Filling

1 lb smoked breakfast sausage
3/4 cup onion, chopped
1 can (4 oz) tomato sauce
1 can (6 oz) tomato paste
1/2 tsp salt
1/4 tsp pepper
1/4 tsp oregano
1/2 cup cheddar cheese, shredded
Parmesan cheese, grated

Pan-fry sausage meat; drain. In some of the drippings brown onion until transparent; add tomato sauce, tomato paste, seasonings, and sausage. Cover and simmer 20 minutes. Pour over fresh crust; top with cheddar cheese. Return to oven until cheese melts. Sprinkle with Parmesan cheese.

Serves 6.

Italian Pizza

1 pkg active dry yeast
1¼ cups warm water
2 tbsp cooking oil
1 tsp salt
4 cups flour
1 can (12 oz) tomato paste
1/2 cup hot water
1 tsp salt
1/8 tsp pepper
1/2 tsp oregano or basil
1 lb mozzarella or Swiss cheese, sliced thin
48 slices salami, cooked

Dissolve yeast in warm water; stir in oil and salt. Mix in flour. Knead on floured board until smooth and elastic, about 15 minutes. Place in greased bowl and brush with oil. Cover and let rise until double in bulk, about 2 hours. Knead lightly and divide into four parts. Roll into approximately 9-inch circles. Place in greased pie pans or on cooky sheets. Dent here and there with fingertips and turn up edges. Brush with oil. Mix tomato paste with water and seasonings. Spread over dough. Add slices of salami and dot with cheese. Bake in 450-degree oven 15 minutes or until dough is brown and crisp.

Makes 2 large or 4 small pizzas.

Imperial Gourmet Pie

1 lb smoked sausage links
4 leeks or 8 green onions
Boiling salted water
Pasty for 2-crust 9-inch pie
2 tbsp butter
2 tbsp flour
Salt to taste
Dash freshly ground white pepper
1/2 cup whipping cream or evaporated
   milk
1 tbsp horseradish
1/2 cup pine nuts or pistachio nuts,
   chopped
Nutmeg

Cut sausage in 1/2-inch slices and sauté; put aside. Cut leeks in 1-inch lengths and split; cover with water and cook until tender. Drain, reserving 1 cup liquid. Line 9-inch piepan with crust. Make sauce, using butter, flour, liquid, seasonings, and cream. Add leeks, horseradish, and nuts with sausage. Pour into shell. Adjust top crust; prick and sprinkle with nutmeg. Bake in 425-degree oven for 30 minutes or until golden.

Serves 6 to 8.

Smoked Summer Sausage Pizza

1 pkg (14 oz) hot roll mix
1/2 cup onion, chopped
1/2 cup ripe olives, sliced
1/4 cup canned mushrooms, sliced
1/2 lb smoked summer sausage, ground
1/2 lb mozzarella cheese, sliced
1 can (6 oz) tomato paste
1 can (8 oz) tomato sauce
1/2 tsp garlic salt
1/2 tsp oregano
1/4 tsp pepper
Olive oil
Parmesan cheese

Prepare roll mix according to package directions. After it has raised, pat into greased pizza pan (or pans, depending on size). Mix remaining ingredients together except olive oil and Parmesan cheese; spread over dough. Brush olive oil over top and sprinkle with Parmesan cheese. Bake in 425-degree oven 15 to 20 minutes.

Makes one 13-inch or 14-inch or two 9-inch pizzas.

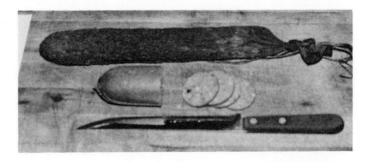

Salads

Smoked Sausage Potato Salad

1/2 cup smoked sausage, chopped
3 cups potatoes, cooked, sliced
3/4 cup celery, sliced
1/2 cup onion, chopped
2 hard-cooked eggs, chopped
1 cup mayonnaise
1/4 cup half and half cream
1 tsp prepared mustard
Salt to taste
1/2 tsp celery seeds

Combine sausage, potatoes, celery, onion, eggs, and mayonnaise; toss. Mix together cream, mustard, salt, and celery seeds. Pour over vegetable mixture and mix carefully. Cover and chill well.

Serves 6.

For a different taste in potato salad, try the Basic Seasoning from the Home Book of Smoke-cooking Meat, Fish & Game," using a small amount mixed with your favorite salad dressing or mayonnaise; add a few dashes of angostura bitters to taste. Let stand under refrigeration for several hours before serving. This gives quite a sharp taste as the flavors mingle.

Smoked Summer Sausage Tropical Salad

2 cups cooked rice, chilled
1 can (13¼ oz) pineapple chunks, drained
1 cup coconut, shredded
1½ cups smoked summer sausage, diced
1 pkg (6 oz) cashew nuts (optional)

Blend all ingredients with the following dressing:

3/4 cup salad dressing
1 tsp sugar
Dash curry powder
Pineapple juice

Chill. Serve on lettuce leaves.

Serves 8 to 10.

Hors d'Oeuvres and Canapés

Butcher's Meat

Smoked Dried Beef Rolls

Spread 1/8-inch-thick slices of smoked dried beef with a mixture of cream cheese and India relish or other sweet relish. Roll; secure with a colored pick and chill.

Smoked Salami Cornucopia

Cut salami very thin. Spread slices with a yellow cheese spread. Roll each slice to form cornucopia. Fasten with wooden picks.

Dinty Moore Celery Sticks

1 cup smoked beef, ground
2 tbsp cream cheese
1/4 cup canned sauerkraut juice
20 3-inch celery stalks
Parsley sprigs

Combine all ingredients, except celery and parsley; mix well. Use smoked beef mixture to fill celery stalks; garnish with parsley.

Rolled Hors d'Oeuvres

Spread 3 or 4 slices of dried smoked beef with a mixture of cream cheese and horseradish. Roll up and fasten with 3 or 4 cocktail picks; chill. Slice between picks to serve.

Smoked Roasted Pâté

2 cups smoked beef, ground
1 tbsp prepared mustard
4 tsp butter or margarine
1 clove garlic, crushed
Basic Seasoning or salt and pepper to
    taste
1/2 cup parsley, chopped
1/2 cup green onion, chopped

Mix ground smoked meat with mustard, butter, crushed garlic, and seasoning. Add parsley and green onion, mixing with hands. If dry, add a little wine, consommé, or beef bouillon; mix to a smooth spreading consistency. Place in a bowl and refrigerate until well chilled. Serve on fancy-cut bread or party crackers.

Tiny hors d'oeuvre sandwiches will not dry out if covered with waxed paper and a damp towel and placed under refrigeration. Remove the towel 20 minutes before serving.

Poultry

Smoked Chicken Canapés

1 carton (12 oz) cottage cheese
1/2 cup smoked chicken, minced
Basic Seasoning or salt and pepper to
    taste
1/2 tsp nutmeg
4 tbsp Parmesan cheese, grated

Blend all ingredients well. Spread on fingers of dark bread. Make these a day ahead and cover with waxed paper, then damp towel.

Variation: Try ground smoked ham and use mustard instead of nutmeg.

Stuffed Eggs

12 hard-cooked eggs
1/2 lb smoked chicken livers
2 tsp green onions, chopped
1 tsp bacon fat
Basic Seasoning or salt and pepper to
    taste
Paprika

Cut hard-cooked eggs in half and remove yolks. Mix egg yolks, smoked livers, green onions, bacon fat, and seasoning to taste. Run through a meat grinder or electric blender. Stuff the egg halves and chill. Sprinkle with paprika.

Makes 24.

Eggs that are several days old will peel better than fresh eggs.

Smoked Chicken Liver Spread or Filling

1/2 cup bacon, cooked, chopped
1/2 cup smoked chicken liver, chopped
Salt, pepper, and cinnamon to taste
1/4 cup whipping cream or mayonnaise

Mix all ingredients, seasoning to taste. Keep under refrigeration until ready to serve. Serve on party crackers and garnish with sweet pickles if desired.

Makes about 1¼ cups.

Winy Smoked Liver Pâté

1/2 cup onion, minced
1/2 cup butter
1/2 cup dry red wine
2 cups smoked chicken livers
2 tsp capers
Basic Seasoning or salt and pepper to
  taste

Sauté the onion in butter until transparent. Add wine; simmer until mixture is reduced by about one-third. Put livers in a bowl with capers and pour over the wine, butter, and onion. Add seasoning and mix well. Run through a food grinder until smooth. Pack paste in a bowl and chill in refrigerator. Serve on thin slices of buttered rye, French bread, or party crackers. Garnish with slices of stuffed olives, diced greens, onion tops, chives, parsley, etc.

Makes about 3½ cups.

Smoked Chicken Liver Balls

4 slices bacon
1 clove garlic, crushed
2 cups smoked chicken livers
Basic Seasoning or salt and pepper to
  taste
1 cup parsley, chopped

Cut up bacon and fry until crisp. Mix together bacon, bacon fat, garlic, smoked chicken livers, and seasoning; run through a meat grinder or electric blender. Shape meat mixture into small balls; roll in chopped parsley. Refrigerate for 2 or 3 hours. Serve on toothpicks, or roll in bread crumbs and cook in hot oil in fondue pot.

Sandwich Loaves

1 loaf white sandwich bread, unsliced
1 loaf whole wheat sandwich bread,
   unsliced
Smoked Chicken, Cottage Cheese, and
   Egg Fillings (see below)
4 pkgs (8 oz ea) cream cheese
1 tbsp onion salad dressing mix

Trim crusts from bread; slice each loaf lengthwise into 5 slices. Prepare one sandwich loaf by layering a white slice, 3/4 cup Smoked Chicken Filling, a whole wheat slice, 1 cup Cottage Cheese Filling, a white slice, 1 cup Egg Filling, a whole wheat slice, 3/4 cup Smoked Chicken Filling, and a white slice. For second loaf repeat layers, but start with whole wheat bread. Chill. Soften cream cheese until smooth; blend in salad dressing mix. Spread over top and sides of loaves. Wrap in waxed paper; chill 3 hours. Serve cold.

Makes 20 slices.

Smoked Chicken Filling

1½ cups smoked chicken, minced
1 cup mayonnaise
1 tbsp onion salad dressing mix
1/4 cup lemon juice
1 cup celery, chopped

Thoroughly combine all ingredients.

Cottage Cheese Filling

1 lb creamed cottage cheese
1 tsp onion salad dressing mix
2 tsp chives, chopped
2 tsp pimiento, chopped

Sieve the cottage cheese and blend in remaining ingredients.

Egg Filling

6 hard-cooked eggs, chopped
6 tbsp mayonnaise
1 tsp onion salad dressing mix
4 to 6 drops Worcestershire sauce
1 tbsp ripe olives, chopped

Thoroughly combine all ingredients.

Smoked Chicken Liver Bourbon Pâté

1 cup butter
1 small onion, chopped
2 cups smoked chicken livers
1½ cups chicken broth, divided
2 tbsp sweet sherry
Salt to taste
1/2 tsp paprika
1/2 tsp tabasco sauce
1/8 tsp allspice
1 clove garlic, minced
1/2 cup Bourbon
1 envelope unflavored gelatin
1 cup walnuts, chopped

In skillet melt butter; add onion and sauté until browned. Add chicken livers and 3/4 cup broth, sherry, salt, paprika, tabasco, allspice, and garlic; cook 5 minutes. Remove from heat and add Bourbon. Soften gelatin in remaining 3/4 cup broth; cook over boiling water until dissolved. Place chicken liver mixture in electric blender; blend until smooth. Stir gelatin and walnuts into chicken mixture. Chill in a 6-cup mold until firm.

Hot Smoked Turkey Hors d'Oeuvres with Gravy

2 lb smoked turkey roast
1 cup fine bread crumbs
1 cup flour
Basic Seasoning or salt and pepper to taste
1 cup buttermilk

Cut turkey into 1/2-inch cubes. Blend bread crumbs, flour, and seasoning. Coat turkey cubes with crumb mixture, then with buttermilk and again in crumb mixture. Fry in deep fat at 375 degrees about 3 minutes, until golden brown. Spear with picks and serve with hot gravy.

Smoked Chicken and Almond Squares

1½ cups smoked chicken, diced
1½ cups toasted almonds, sliced
1/2 cup mayonnaise
1/4 cup crushed pineapple, well drained
1 tbsp onion, minced
1 tsp lemon juice
Salt to taste
1/4 tsp curry powder
1/2 tsp poultry seasoning
12 slices white bread, toasted
Butter
Olives

Mix together chicken, almonds, mayonnaise, pineapple, onion, lemon juice, and seasonings. Refrigerate overnight. Before serving, bring chicken mixture to room temperature. Toast bread, trim crusts; butter slices. Spread chicken mixture on six slices toast. Cover with remaining toast. Cut each sandwich into 4 squares. Top each with an olive on a pick.

Makes 24 squares.

Japanese Ginger Chicken

1/2 cup chicken broth
1 egg, slightly beaten
1/2 cup bread crumbs
1½ cups smoked chicken, ground
Salt to taste
1/2 tsp monosodium glutamate
1 tbsp scallions, chopped
1/2 tsp lemon juice
1/4 tsp fresh ginger, grated

In a medium bowl pour chicken broth and egg over crumbs and let stand until moistened. Add remaining ingredients, mixing well. Form into small balls, using 1 rounded tsp for each. Place on a greased baking sheet and bake in a preheated 375-degree oven for 20 minutes. Serve hot with Japanese Sauce (see below).

Makes 24 appetizers.

Japanese Sauce

1/4 cup soy sauce
2 tbsp sake
1/4 cup water
1 tbsp chopped scallions
1 tbsp ginger
1 tsp cornstarch

Combine all ingredients in a saucepan and cook, stirring constantly, until mixture thickens slightly and comes to a boil. Simmer 1 minute. Serve warm.

Sandwich Loaf

1½-lb loaf sandwich bread, unsliced
Soft butter
9 oz cream cheese
Milk
Egg, Smoked Chicken, and Cheese Fillings
   (see below)

Remove crusts from bread; cut lengthwise into 4 slices. Spread slices with soft butter. Beat cream cheese and milk until evenly mixed and soft enough to spread. Set aside. Spread Egg Filling on first slice of bread. Cover with second slice and spread with the Smoked Chicken Filling. Cover with third slice and spread with Cheese Filling. Cover with the fourth slice of bread, buttered side down, and frost the entire loaf with cream cheese, leaving cheese in rough swirls. Chill loaf several hours before serving.

Serves 10.

Egg Filling

4 hard-cooked eggs, chopped
1/3 cup cooked bacon, chopped, or 1/3
   cup stuffed olives, chopped
Few drops Worcestershire sauce
Cream or salad dressing

Combine eggs, bacon, and Worcestershire and moisten with cream.

Smoked Chicken Filling

1 cup smoked chicken, ground
2 to 4 tbsp celery, chopped
1/2 cup almonds, ground
Salt and lemon juice to taste
Salad dressing

Combine smoked chicken, celery, and almonds; season with salt and lemon juice and moisten with dressing.

Cheese Filling

6 oz pimiento cheese
Salad dressing

Moisten pimiento cheese with salad dressing.

Wild Game

Smoked Venison Pâté

2 cups smoked venison, ground
1 small onion, minced
2 hard-cooked eggs, minced
1/2 cup almonds, ground
Basic Seasoning or salt and pepper to
 taste
Dash tabasco sauce
2 tbsp cognac
Mayonnaise to bind
Olives for garnish

Combine all ingredients, except mayonnaise and garnish. Bind with mayonnaise until a stiff paste is formed. Place in a bowl and decorate with olives; chill. Serve with party crackers.

Smoked Venison Pâté Maison

1 cup smoked venison, diced
1/4 cup carrots, chopped
Basic Seasoning or salt and pepper to
 taste
2 tbsp butter or margarine, melted
2 tbsp brandy or dry sherry

Put smoked venison and carrots through a meat grinder, using the finest blade. Season to taste and add remaining ingredients. Pack in a small crock or bowl to serve with cocktail crackers.

Smoked Venison Rolls

1 pkg (8 oz) cream cheese, softened
2 tbsp horseradish
Thin slices smoked venison

Combine cream cheese and horseradish; spread on slices of smoked venison. Roll up tightly and fasten with cocktail pick; chill.

Seafood

Smoked Shrimp Scampi

1/8 tsp garlic, minced
2 tbsp parsley flakes
1/2 cup white table wine
4 tbsp butter or margarine
2 cups smoked shrimp

In skillet or saucepan sauté garlic and parsley in wine and butter. Heat to simmering; add smoked shrimp and cook over low heat until heated through, about 5 minutes. Serve with toast squares or rice as a light main course. Or serve from chafing dish with cocktail picks as hot hor d'oeuvre.

Celery Stuffed with Smoked Fish

1 pkg (3 oz) cream cheese
2 tbsp mayonnaise
Salt to taste
1 cup smoked fish, flaked
6 stalks crisp celery
Lettuce
2 cups grapefruit segments, chilled
French dressing

Mash cheese. Add mayonnaise, salt, and smoked fish; blend well. Pack grooves of celery with mixture; cut into 3/4-inch slices. Arrange on lettuce with grapefruit segments. Sprinkle with French dressing.

Smoked Fish Puffs

2 cups sifted flour
3 tsp baking powder
1 cup cold milk
1 egg, beaten
1/2 lb smoked fish, flaked fine
Salt to taste
Parsley
Lemon wedges

Sift together sifted flour and baking powder. Add milk and egg; beat until mixture is well blended. Add smoked fish and salt to taste. Blend well, adding more fish if mixture is too soft to drop from a teaspoon. Drop into hot deep fat from a teaspoon, dipped in hot water, and fry until the puffs are golden brown; drain. Serve on a bed of curled parsley garnished with lemon wedges.

Makes about 3 dozen.

California Smoked Shrimp Cocktail

1 cup bottled cocktail sauce
1/3 cup red table wine
1/4 cup cream
1 tsp lemon juice
Salt to taste
2 cups smoked shrimp

Mix sauce, wine, cream, lemon juice, and salt. Add smoked shrimp; chill well. Serve in cocktail glasses. If smoked shrimp are large, cut into small pieces.

Smoked Fish Canapés

6 thin slices party pumpernickel
Butter or margarine
12 slices smoked fish (4 oz)
1/4 cup sour cream
1 tsp onion, chopped
Capers, drained

Spread bread with butter; cut each slice in half. Lay one slice smoked fish on each half. Combine sour cream and onion and dollop over smoked fish; garnish with capers.

Makes 12.

Smoked Oyster Puffs

16 slices party rye bread
1/4 cup mayonnaise
2 tbsp green onion, sliced
8 slices (8 oz) Swiss cheese
16 smoked oysters

Toast bread on both sides. Combine mayonnaise and green onion. Spread on one side of toast slices. Cut out 2 rounds of cheese to fit toast from each cheese slice. Place a smoked oyster on each bread round; then top with cheese round. Broil 3 to 4 inches from heat until cheese is puffy and golden.

Makes 16.

Smoked Fish Flake Cocktail

2 cups smoked fish, flaked
1 tbsp lemon juice
2 tbsp sweet-sour gherkins
1 tbsp pickled beets, chopped
Basic Seasoning or salt and pepper to
    taste
Dash tabasco sauce (optional)
2 tbsp mayonnaise
Thousand Island dressing

Have all ingredients well chilled. Combine smoked fish, lemon juice, gherkins, and pickled beets. Season to taste and, if desired, dash with tabasco sauce. Gently blend with mayonnaise. Lightly cover with Thousand Island dressing.

Serves 6.

Smoked Fish and Cheese Dip

1½ cups smoked fish, flaked
2 pkgs (3 oz ea) cream cheese
1 clove garlic, minced
2 tbsp Worcestershire sauce
1 tbsp lemon juice
3 tbsp onion, minced
Salt to taste
Strips of pimiento

Mash smoked fish with cheese; blend in garlic, Worcestershire, lemon juice, onion, and salt. Chill several hours before serving to blend flavors. Serve garnished with pimiento strips. Use as dip for crackers or potato or corn chips.

Makes 2¼ cups.

Smoked Oyster Dip

1 pkg (8 oz) cream cheese
2 cups sour cream
2 cups smoked oysters, grated
Pinch salt

Cream cheese with sour cream; add oysters and season to taste. Chill.

Makes 1½ cups.

Smoked Clam Appetizer Dip

1 clove garlic, peeled
2 tsp lemon juice
Salt to taste
1/2 cup smoked clams, diced
1 pkg (8 oz) cream cheese
1½ tsp Worcestershire sauce
Dash pepper

Rub mixing bowl with garlic. Blend remaining ingredients in bowl. Use as a dip for crackers, potato chips, or corn chips. If thinner mixture is desired, use a little cooking oil.

Makes about 1½ cups.

Smoked Fish Dip

1 to 2 tbsp milk
1 pkg (3 oz) cream cheese
1/3 cup smoked fish
1 tbsp parsley, snipped
Dash garlic powder

Gradually blend milk and cheese until smooth. Stir in fish, parsley, and garlic powder. Chill. Serve with crackers.

Makes 2/3 cup.

Smoked Salmon and Celery Rolls

Spread thinly sliced smoked salmon with cream cheese. Roll around 2-inch stalks of crisp celery.

Pickled Smoked Seafood

4 cups vinegar
2 tbsp mixed pickling spices
1 tsp dry mustard
1 small onion, diced
1 clove garlic, minced, or 1 tbsp liquid
   garlic
2 tbsp salt
3 cups water
3 lb smoked shrimp, fish, or scallops, or
   3 qt smoked oysters

Combine vinegar, spices, mustard, onion, garlic, salt, and water in a saucepan; bring to boil and simmer 5 minutes. Pour over smoked fish and refrigerate 24 hours in a nonmetal container.

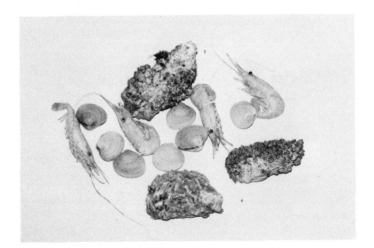

Tomato Smoked Shrimp Frappé

3/4 cup mixed vegetable or tomato juice
2 tsp Worcestershire sauce
1/4 tsp salt
5 or 6 smoked shrimp
1/3 cup lemon juice
1 can (12½ oz) jellied madrilene

Place all ingredients in blender; cover; blend well. Pour into shallow pan. Freeze, stirring occasionally, until mixture has frozen to a mush. Spoon into sherbet glasses; garnish with additional shrimp and tomato slices and serve with lemon wedge, if desired.

Serves 3 to 4.

Cheddar Smoked Fish Canapés

1 cup smoked fish, flaked
2 cups cheddar cheese, grated
2 tbsp dry vermouth
Pepper
6 slices toast, quartered

Mix together smoked fish, cheese, vermouth, and pepper. Spread on toast and place in preheated 350-degree oven until hot.

Makes 24.

Smoked Shrimp Cocktail

You may serve smoked shrimp in cups scooped from oranges, grapefruit, raw tomatoes, or green peppers.

Smoked seafood may be blended with cubed avocado meat.

Eggs and Cheese

Pears and Apples with Smoked Cheese Dip

2 tbsp butter or margarine
3 tbsp flour
1/2 tsp dry mustard
2 cups milk or light cream, scalded
3 cups smoked cheese, shredded
1/2 cup dry sauterne
1 tbsp cognac or brandy
Pears and apples, about 4 each
French bread chunks (optional)

In saucepan melt butter. Blend in flour and mustard; cook until bubbly. Gradually stir in milk and cook, stirring occasionally until thickened. Add cheese and stir over medium heat until melted. Blend in sauterne and cognac. Place mixture over a small candle warmer and dip wedges of pears and apples or chunks of bread into sauce. Stir occasionally; thin if necessary with warmed milk or light cream.

Makes about 4 cups.

Pickled Smoked Eggs

1 cup red table wine
1¼ cups canned beet juice
1½ cups vinegar
2 tbsp mixed pickling spices
1 small onion, diced
1½ tsp salt
Few grains white pepper
2 garlic cloves, crushed
12 smoked eggs

Combine all ingredients except eggs in saucepan; bring to boil and simmer 5 minutes. Pour over smoked eggs and refrigerate 24 hours in a nonmetal container.

If you shake eggs vigorously before boiling, the yolks will remain in the center when hard-cooked.

Smoked Moss Balls

1 pkg (8 oz) cream cheese
1/4 to 1/2 lb blue cheese, crumbled
1/4 lb smoked cheddar cheese, grated
1 small onion, finely chopped
1 tbsp Worcestershire sauce
1/2 cup pecans, chopped
Parsley, chopped

Place cheeses in mixing bowl and let stand at room temperature until softened. Beat until smooth. Add onion and Worcestershire sauce and beat well. Stir in pecans. Chill 3 to 4 hours. Roll cheese mixture into one large ball; chill and roll in parsley. Put on serving plate and chill 2 hours or until firm. Serve the cheese ball with a variety of party crackers.

Smoked Egg Dip

12 smoked eggs, chopped
2 tbsp soft butter
1 tbsp lemon juice
2 tsp prepared mustard
1 tbsp Worcestershire sauce
2 drops tabasco sauce
1½ tsp salt
1 tsp onion, dried, minced
1/4 tsp pepper
3/4 cup mayonnaise

Combine all ingredients and blend until smooth. Chill at least 4 hours. Before serving whip to soften.

Makes 1 quart.

When hard-cooking eggs, begin with water to cover that is the same temperature as the eggs. Add a dash of salt or vinegar to prevent cracking and make peeling easier. Bring to boiling over medium heat. Remove from heat and let stand, covered, about 15 minutes. Drain and cover with cold water or ice water in order to aid peeling and prevent a dark ring from appearing around the yolk.

Canapé Spreads and Butters

All of these spreads and butters are prepared as follows; Cream butter or cream cheese thoroughly. Grind, mince, or chop fish, meat, or vegetables and combine with the seasonings and butter, mayonnaise, cream, cream cheese, etc. Spread on toast rounds or crackers and garnish appropriately or use as a base for sandwich fillings.

Smoked Fish (Shrimp) and Cheese

1 cup smoked fish (shrimp), flaked
1 cup sharp cheese spread
Mayonnaise to bind

At Christmas time, color the above spread with green food coloring. Use a cookie cutter to cut Christmas tree shapes from thin slices of rye bread. Spread with green spread and decorate with slivers of carrots, pickled beets or red pimiento for candles. This makes an attractive centerpiece for an hors d'oeuvre or canapé tray.

The above spread is very delicious and has a very special tang when made with pickled smoked foods prepared as directed under recipe for Pickled Smoked Seafood.

Smoked Clam Spread

1 clove garlic
1 pkg (8 oz) cream cheese
1 tsp lemon juice
1 tsp Worcestershire sauce
Basic Seasoning or salt and pepper to
  taste
1/2 cup cucumber, peeled, chopped
1/2 cup smoked clams, minced
1 tbsp vegetable oil

Rub mixing bowl with clove of garlic before combining ingredients.

Smoked Venison Casserole

Pizza Plate

An interesting way to serve hors d'oeuvres is to use a cabbage head as in the picture. Hollow out the top of the head to hold your favorite dip; cut a slice off the bottom so that it will sit level. Place on a bed of brilliant green or red cabbage leaves. Stick picks with hors d'oeuvres around the cabbage head. In the picture we have used smoked fish, smoked shrimp, and smoked octopus. The hors d'oeuvres are easily replaced as used from the cabbage head.

Head of Cabbage with Smoked Seafood

Smoked Fish Butter

1 cup smoked fish, flaked
1 cup butter
1 tbsp lemon juice
Salt to taste
Dash paprika

Many spreads made with smoked salmon, shrimp, smelt, octopus, scallops, etc. may be successfully canned. Many readers may be skeptical that a spread which has cheese and mayonnaise can be canned. However, when such spreads are removed from the pressure cooker after processing (for small jars, process at 10 pounds pressure for 75 minutes), the oils and fats from these products will have separated and risen to the top. Just place these spreads on your canned goods shelf, and very shortly the oils will be absorbed back into the foods. When opened, they may need more mayonnaise to make them of spreading consistency.

Smoked Fish Spread

1½ cups smoked fish, flaked
1 cup sour cream
1 envelope green onion dip mix
1 tsp Worcestershire sauce

Smoked Fish and Ham

1/2 cup smoked fish, flaked
1/2 cup deviled ham
Mayonnaise to bind

Smoked Salmon Butter

1/2 cup smoked salmon, flaked
1/2 cup soft butter
1/2 tsp white pepper

Smoked Shrimp Butter

1 cup butter
1 cup smoked shrimp, minced
Salt to taste
Dash paprika
1 tbsp lemon juice

Smoked Chicken and Sharp Cheese Spread

1 cup smoked chicken, ground
1 cup sharp cheese spread
Mayonnaise

Smoked Chicken and Pineapple

3/4 cup smoked chicken, minced
1/3 cup crushed pineapple
3 tbsp mayonnaise

Toasted Almonds and Smoked Poultry

1 cup smoked poultry, minced
1/2 cup toasted almonds, chopped
1 tsp onion, grated
1/2 tsp curry powder
1/2 cup mayonnaise

Sweet Pickle and Smoked Poultry

1 cup smoked poultry, ground
1/4 cup cream
3 tbsp sweet pickle relish

Smoked Chicken Livers and Bacon

1 cup smoked chicken livers, mashed
2 tbsp cooked bacon, minced
4 drops tabasco sauce
1 tbsp lemon juice

Smoked Chicken Livers with Onion

3/4 cup smoked chicken livers, mashed
2 tbsp chicken fat
1/3 cup sautéed onion, chopped
Basic Seasoning or salt and pepper to
   taste

Smoked Turkey and Egg

3/4 cup smoked turkey, chopped
1/3 cup hard-cooked eggs, chopped
Basic Seasoning or salt and pepper to
   taste
1 tsp piccalilli
3 tbsp mayonnaise

Smoked Turkey and Mushrooms

3/4 cup smoked turkey, chopped

1/3 cup mushrooms, chopped

3 tbsp capers, chopped

3 tbsp mayonnaise

1 tsp mustard

Smoked Chicken Giblets with Almonds

1 cup smoked chicken giblets, chopped

1 tsp onion, chopped

1/2 cup mayonnaise

1/2 cup almonds, toasted, chopped

1/2 tsp curry powder

Smoked Chicken Liver and Shrimp

1/2 cup smoked chicken livers, ground

1/4 onion, minced

Chili sauce to blend

1/2 cup smoked shrimp, ground

1/2 green pepper, minced

Smoke-roasted Cured Meat* Spreads

1 cup smoked cured meat, ground
1 cup sharp cheese spread
Mayonnaise to bind

Smoked Liverwurst Spread

1/2 cup smoked liverwurst, mashed
3 tbsp chili sauce
1/4 cup stuffed olives, chopped
Few drops lemon juice

Smoked Liver Sausage

1 cup smoked liver sausage
1 cup cream cheese
2 tbsp pickle relish
2 slices bacon, cooked, crumbled

*You may use any of the following red meats: antelope, bear, beef, caribou, elk, moose, reindeer, or venison.

Summer Sausage and Cheese

1 cup smoked summer sausage, ground
1 cup sharp cheese spread
Mayonnaise to bind

To cut extra-thin, well-shaped slices of bread for party sandwiches, freeze the bread first.

Note: Some of the following butters do not have a smoked food ingredient, but can readily be used as a base on canapés and topped with your favorite smoked meats or fish.

Chive Butter

1/2 cup butter
1/4 cup chives, chopped
4 drops Worcestershire sauce

Horseradish Butter

1/2 cup butter
1/4 cup grated horseradish

Anchovy Butter

1 cup butter
1/2 cup anchovies, minced, or 4 tbsp
   anchovy paste
2 tsp lemon juice
4 drops onion juice

Smoked Herring or Lobster Butter

1 cup butter
1/2 cup smoked herring or lobster
2 tsp lemon juice
4 drops onion juice

Blue Cheese Butter

1/2 cup blue cheese, crumbled
1/2 cup butter

Smoked Smelt Butter

1/2 cup butter
1/2 cup smoked smelt, flaked
Cayenne pepper
Lemon juice
Salt to taste

Garlic Butter

1/2 cup butter
1 small clove garlic, pureed
Cayenne pepper or Worcestershire sauce
   to taste

This is an excellent accent to beef or lamb.

Mustard Butter

1/2 cup butter
1/4 cup prepared mustard

Smoked Ham Butter

1/2 cup butter
1/2 cup smoked ham
2 hard-cooked eggs, chopped
Dash pepper

Smoked Egg Butter

1/2 cup butter
4 smoked egg yolks
Few grains cayenne pepper
6 drops Worcestershire sauce

Cheese Butter

1/2 cup butter
1/4 cup Parmesan cheese, grated, or 1/2
  cup sharp cheese spread

Pimiento Butter

1/2 cup butter
1/4 cup pimiento, mashed
2 tsp India relish, drained

Olive Butter

1/4 cup butter
2 tbsp olives, chopped
1/4 tsp lemon juice

Chili Butter

1/4 cup butter
2 tbsp chili sauce

Poppy Seed Butter

1/2 cup butter
1/2 cup hot poppy seeds or caraway

Recipe Locator

A Guide to Using Ingredients

Note: This guide does not contain entries for the various smoked meats, poultry, and seafoods, since they can easily be found under the appropriate heads. For instance, recipes using beef, veal, and pork will be found under Smoked Butcher's Meat; recipes using chicken, turkey, and duck, under Smoke-roasted Poultry and Game Birds; recipes using venison, squirrel, and rabbit, under Smoke-roasted Wild Game; recipes using fish, shrimp, and oysters, under Smoked Seafood, and recipes using sausage, under Sausage.

APPLESAUCE:
Applesauce Moose Loaf, 88
Smoked Sausage, Apple, and Yam Casserole, 181
Smoked Sausage-Apple-Noodle Casserole, 182

ARTICHOKE HEARTS, CANNED:
Chef's Salad, 73

ASPARAGUS:
Smoked Turkey Supreme, 79

ASPARAGUS, COOKED:
Smoked Shrimp and Vegetable Salad, 162

ASPARAGUS SOUP:
Smoked Fish Fritters, 141

AVOCADO:
Avocado Filled With Smoked Fish, 148
Seafood Soufflé Salad, 160
Smoked Fish Fruit Salad with Avocado-Orange Garnish, 148
Smoked Rabbit and Avocado Newburg, 110
Smoked Salmon Pensacola, 139
Smoked Shrimp Salad Supreme, 159
Smoked Squirrel Salad, 102

AVOCADO DIP:
Smoked Fish Salad Loaf, 151

BACON:
Egg Filling for Sandwich Loaf, 195
Hearty Smoked Fish Chowder, 131
Onions with Smoked Rabbit Stuffing, 88
Peppered Smoked Fish and Eggs, 142
Scrambled Eggs with Smoked Fish, 141
Smoked Chicken Liver Balls, 191
Smoked Chicken Liver Spread or Filling, 191
Smoked Chicken Livers and Bacon, 212
Smoked Fish Hash, 176
Smoked Fish Pilaf, 145
Smoked Liver Sausage, 214
Smoked Moose Hash, 98
Smoked Octopus Chowder, 132
Smoked Raccoon and Spaghetti, 109
Smoked Squirrel Salad, 102
Smoked Turkey Club Sandwiches, 75
Smoked Venison Biscuit Roll, 100

BAMBOO SHOOTS:
Lobster and Smoked Chicken Cantonese, 44
Smoked Beef Sukiyaki, 15
Smoked Fish Sukiyaki, 128

BANANAS:
Chilled Smoked Chicken and Fruit Salad, 63
Fruity Smoked Chicken Salad, 65
Smoked Fish Fruit Salad, 148

BEAN SPROUTS:
Chinese Chicken Casserole, 38
Chinese Duck with Almond, 45
Chinese Garden Smoked Rabbit Salad, 102
Mandarin Salad, 20
Smoked Beef Chop Suey, 14
Smoked Chicken Chow Mein, 44
Smoked Fish Chow Mein, 126
Smoked Fish Fried Rice, 128
Smoked Fish Sukiyaki, 128
Smoked Rabbit Chop Suey, 92
Smoked Shrimp Fried Rice, 129

BEANS, FRENCH-STYLE (FROZEN):
Hearty Smoked Turkey Soup, 77

BEANS, GREEN (COOKED):
Curried Smoked Mountain Sheep Loaf, 84
Smoked Rabbit Pie with Buttermilk Crust, 101

BEANS, ITALIAN GREEN (FROZEN):
Beef Casserole, Roman Style, 13
Chinese Smoked Chicken, 43

BEEF STOCK:
Spaghetti with Smoked Chicken Livers, 81

BEER:
Smoked Venison in Barbecue Sauce, 87

BEET JUICE:
Pickled Smoked Eggs, 203

BEETS, CANNED:
Scandinavian Smoked Fish Salad, 161

BEETS, COOKED:
Scandinavian Apple Salad, 20

BEETS, PICKLED:
Smoked Fish Flake Cocktail, 199

BISCUIT MIX:
Smoked Chicken Enchiladas, 81
Smoked Squirrel Biscuit Roll, 99
Smoked Summer Sausage Pizza, 185

BISCUITS:
Beef Casserole, Roman Style, 13
Smoked Beef Pub Pasties, 18
Smoked Chicken Shortcakes, 51
Smoked Fish Biscuit Loaf, 116

BOUILLON:
Curried Venison, Seattle Style, 94
Smoked Chicken Livers Sautéed, 61
Smoked Duck Meatballs, 82
Smoked Fish And Cucumber Mousse, 155

BOUILLON, BEEF:
Smoked Beef Chop Suey for a Party, 14
Smoked Beef Tetrazzini, 12
Smoked Sausage Chowder, 182
Smoked Tongue in Aspic, 21
Smoked Veal Curry, 24

BOUILLON, CHEESE:
Herb Crust Smoked Turkey Pie, 50

BOUILLON, CHICKEN:
Baked Smoked Rabbit Hash, 98
Chicken and Pineapple Salad, 66
Cold Smoked Fish Soup, 133
Curried Smoked Rabbit with Rice, 97
Fancy Smoked Fish Chowder, 132
Ground Smoked Turkey or Chicken Loaf, 36
Herb Crust Smoked Turkey Pie, 50
Risotto with Smoked Shrimp, 143
Smoked Chicken and Lobster Casserole, 37
Smoked Chicken Curry, 59
Smoked Chicken Pilaf, 57
Smoked Duck Curry with Sour Cream, 57
Smoked Fish Burgers, 168
Smoked Fish Risotto with Green Peppers, 145
Smoked Pheasant à la King, 48
Smoked Pheasant Delight, 61
Smoked Pheasant Meringue Pie, 52
Smoked Rabbit Chop Suey, 92
Smoked Shrimp Chowder, 133
Smoked Squirrel Supreme, 96

Smoked Turkey and Lemon Rice Casserole, 32
Smoked Turkey Gobbler Soup, 78
Smoked Turkey with Wild Rice, 28
Southern Smoked Squirrel, 90
Won Ton Soup, 23

BOUILLON, TURKEY:
Smoked Turkey and Rice Casserole with Olives, 37

BOUILLON, VEGETABLE:
Smoked Fish Mediterranean, 124

BOURBON:
Smoked Chicken Liver Bourbon Pâté, 193

BRANDY:
Pears and Apples with Smoked Cheese Dip, 203
Smoked Fish Salad with Roquefort, 152
Smoked Fish Zarzuela, 143
Smoked Venison Pâté Maison, 196

BRAZIL NUTS:
Smoked Chicken or Turkey Divan with Nuts, 29
Smoked Chicken with Nuts and Spaghetti, 28

BREAD:
Sandwich Loaf, 195
Sandwich Loaves, 192
Smoked Chicken and Almond Squares, 194

BREAD, FRENCH:
Smoked Fish Boat Dinner, 177
Smoked Fish Salad Loaf, 151

BREAD, PUMPERNICKEL:
Smoked Fish Canapés, 199
Smoked Fish Sandwich, 169

BREAD, RYE:
Smoked Oyster Puffs, 199

BREAD, VIENNA:
Smoked Fish Salad Loaf, 151

BREAD, WHOLE WHEAT:
Sandwich Loaves, 192

BREAD CRUMBS:
Apples with Smoked Chicken Stuffing, 80
Baked Smoked Rabbit Hash, 98
Baked Smoked Squirrel Loaf, 85
Chicken or Turkey Tetrazzini, 35
Country Smoked Chicken Loaf, 36
Curried Smoked Mountain Sheep Loaf, 84
Easy-to-Fix Smoked Fish Loaf, 124
Elegant Smoked Fish Loaf, 124
Elegant Stuffed Peppers, 125
Frosted Smoked Salmon Loaf, 119
Ground Smoked Turkey or Chicken Loaf, 36
Hot Smoked Turkey Hors d'Oeuvres with Gravy, 193
Japanese Ginger Chicken, 194
Japanese Mandarin Smoked Fish Loaf, 119
Peppers with Smoked Fish Stuffing, 125
Savory Smoked Fish Loaf, 122
Scalloped Eggs, 13
Scalloped Smoked Fish, 120
Smoked Chicken and Macaroni Casserole, 29
Smoked Chicken and Vegetable Casserole, 26
Smoked Chicken Ring or Loaf, 40
Smoked Duck Meatballs, 82
Smoked Fish and Noodle Bake, 117
Smoked Fish Burgers, 168
Smoked Fish Cakes, 147
Smoked Fish Croquettes, 146
Smoked Fish Loaf Delight, 117

CELERY (cont.)

Smoked Salmon Mousse with Horseradish, 157
Smoked Salmon Mousse with Mustard, 164
Smoked Salmon Pensacola, 139
Smoked Salmon Salad, 163
Smoked Sausage Chowder, 182
Smoked Sausage Potato Salad, 186
Smoked Shrimp and Vegetable Salad, 162
Smoked Shrimp and Waffles, 139
Smoked Shrimp Bisque, 130
Smoked Shrimp Salad, 163
Smoked Shrimp Salad Sandwich, 175
Smoked Shrimp Salad Supreme, 159
Smoked Shrimp Tahiti, 144
Smoked Smelt Salad, 166
Smoked Squirrel Salad Loaf, 106
Smoked Turkey and Tomato Mold, 72
Smoked Turkey Chow Mein, 45
Smoked Turkey Cranberry Mold, 64
Smoked Turkey Gobbler Soup, 78
Smoked Turkey in Curry, 60
Smoked Turkey Pasty, 53
Smoked Turkey Salad with Tomatoes, 74
Smoked Turkey Sukiyaki, 42
Smoked Turkey Supreme on Corn Bread, 60
Smoked Veal Curry, 24
Smoked Venison and Vegetable Salad, 105
Smoked Venison Surprise Salad, 106
Superb Smoked Chicken Liver Filling, 76
Sweet and Sour Dressing, 150
Tomatoes Stuffed with Smoked Chicken Salad, 74
Won Ton Soup, 23

CELERY SEED:
Smoked Sausage Potato Salad, 186

CELERY SOUP, CREAM OF:
Chipper Smoked Fish Loaf with Fluffy Lemon Sauce, 115
Elegant Smoked Fish Loaf, 122
Smoked Catfish Casserole, 115
Smoked Catfish Soufflé, 125
Smoked Fish and Noodle Bake, 117
Smoked Fish and Noodle Casserole, 121

CELERY TOPS:
Smoked Beef Tongue Burgundy, 24

CHEESE:
American Smoked Chicken Chop Suey, 43
Smoked Chicken and Noodle Casserole, 26
Smoked Fish Cheese Loaf, 122
Smoked Liver Burgers, 22
Smoked Turkey Supreme, 79

CHEESE, AMERICAN
Baked Smoked Fish Puffs, 118
Beef Casserole, Roman Style, 13
Chipped Smoked Beef Casserole, 13
Open-Face Broiled Smoked Fish Sandwich, 169
Smoked Chicken Enchiladas, 81
Smoked Duck Casserole Supreme, 37
Smoked Fish and Noodle Bake, 117
Smoked Fish and Noodle Casserole, 121
Smoked Fish Biscuit Loaf, 116
Smoked Fish Boat Dinner, 177
Smoked Rabbit Macaroni Casserole, 86
Smoked Sausage Toast, 183

CHEESE, BLUE:
Blue Cheese Butter, 217
Smoked Goose Elegante, 39
Smoked Moss Balls, 204

CHEESE, CHEDDAR:
Cheddar Smoked Fish Canapés, 202
Hot Smoked Turkey Salad, 41
Smoked Breakfast Sausage Pizza, 184
Smoked Chicken and Lobster Casserole, 37
Smoked Chicken and Macaroni Casserole, 29
Smoked Chicken and Noodle Casserole with Mushrooms, 38
Smoked Chicken and Potato Florentine, 30
Smoked Chipped Beef and Corn Casserole, 12
Smoked Duck Almandine, 40
Smoked Fish and Cheddar Sandwich, 175
Smoked Fish Casserole with Cheese Swirls, 118
Smoked Fish Loaf Delight, 117
Smoked Fish Mediterranean, 124
Smoked Fish Patties, 176
Smoked Moss Balls, 204
Smoked Salad Loaf, 151
Smoked Salami and Cheese Raisin Bread, 183
Smoked Sausage-Apple-Noodle Casserole, 182
Smoked Sausage Oven Pancakes, 180
Smoked Turkey and Rice Casserole with Olives, 37
Smoked Turkey Pie, 49
Smoked Turkey Spaghetti Casserole, 28
Smoked Venison Casserole, 89

CHEESE, GRATED:
Smoked Fish au Gratin, 114
Smoked Rabbit Sandwich Spread with Olives, 107

CHEESE, ITALIAN:
Smoked Venison Pizza, 101

CHEESE, MONTEREY JACK:
Smoked Venison Pizza, 101

CHEESE, MOZZARELLA:
Italian Pizza, 184
Smoked Chicken and Spaghetti, 31
Smoked Fish, Cheese, and Tomato on Bed of Potato, 114
Smoked Sausage Lasagne, 181
Smoked Summer Sausage Pizza, 185

CHEESE, PARMESAN:
Cheese Butter, 219
Chicken or Turkey Tetrazzini, 35
Deluxe Smoked Venison Sandwiches, 108
Hot Squirrel Casserole, 91
Lemony Smoked Fish Crepes, 140
Smoked Beef Tetrazzini, 12
Smoked Breakfast Sausage Pizza, 184
Smoked Chicken Canapés, 190
Smoked Chicken Hashed in Cream, 56
Smoked Chicken or Turkey and Rice Curry, 28
Smoked Chicken or Turkey Divan with Nuts, 29
Smoked Chicken Tamale Pie, 30
Smoked Elk Florentine, 111
Smoked Goose Elegante, 39
Smoked Pheasant Meringue Pie, 52
Smoked Raccoon and Spaghetti, 109
Smoked Sausage Lasagne, 181
Smoked Turkey or Chicken Almandine, 27
Smoked Turkey or Chicken for a Party, 31
Smoked Turkey Pasty, 53
Spaghetti with Smoked Chicken Livers, 81

CHEESE, PIMIENTO:
Cheese Filling for Sandwich Loaf, 195

CHEESE, ROQUEFORT:
Smoked Chicken Liver Salad, 66
Smoked Fish Salad with Roquefort, 152
Smoked Squirrel Salad, 102

CHEESE, SHARP:
Smoked Fish Nuggets, 178

CHEESE, SMOKED:
Pears and Apples with Smoked Cheese Dip, 203

CHEESE, SWISS:
Baked Smoked Chicken Salad, 30
Chef's Salad, 73
Chef's Salad Bowl, 74
Italian Pizza, 184
Lemony Smoked Fish Crepes, 140
Open-Face Broiled Smoked Fish Sandwich, 169
Savannah Smoked Rabbit, 109
Scrambled Eggs and Smoked Fish on Toast, 142
Smoked Chicken and Noodle Casserole With Mushrooms, 38
Smoked Chicken with Nuts and Spaghetti, 28
Smoked Oyster Puffs, 199
Smoked Salami and Cheese Raisin Bread, 183
Smoked Turkey Pie, 49

CHEESE SAUCE:
Smoked Turkey Pasty, 53

CHEESE SOUP, CHEDDAR:
Smoked Turkey or Chicken à la King with Cheese and Pimiento, 46

CHEESE SPREAD:
Cheese Butter, 219
Smoked Chicken and Sharp Cheese Spread, 210
Smoked Fish Croquettes, 146
Smoked Fish (Shrimp) and Cheese, 205
Smoked Salami Cornucopia, 188
Summer Sausage and Cheese, 215

CHERRIES, BING:
Smoked Pheasant and Rice Almandine, 39

CHICKEN CONSOMMÉ:
Creamed Smoked Rabbit, 95
Smoked Duck with Red Wine, 61

CHICKEN SOUP, CREAM OF:
Good Creamed Chicken, 47
Smoked Catfish Casserole, 115
Smoked Chicken and Macaroni Casserole, 29
Smoked Chicken Curry in a Hurry, 57
Smoked Chicken Shortcakes, 51
Smoked Chicken with Nuts and Spaghetti, 28
Smoked Goose Elegante, 39
Smoked Turkey Crepes, 49

CHICKEN STOCK:
Baked Smoked Squirrel Loaf, 85
Oklahoma Squirrel Pie, 87
Risotto with Smoked Shrimp, 143
Smoked Chicken Bisque, 79
Smoked Chicken Chop Suey, 41
Smoked Chicken Hash, 55
Smoked Chicken Pie with Sweet Potato Crust, 53
Smoked Chicken Salad Mold, 72
Smoked Fish Risotto with Green Pepper, 145
Smoked Fish Sukiyaki, 128
Smoked Pheasant à la King, 48
Smoked Pheasant Delight, 61

CHICKEN WITH RICE SOUP:
Smoked Fish Casserole with Cheese Swirls, 118

CHICORY:
Smoked Squirrel Salad, 102

CHILI POWDER:
American Smoked Chicken Chop Suey, 43
Smoked Chicken Enchiladas, 81
Smoked Rabbit Tamale Pie, 86

CHILI SAUCE:
Chili Butter, 220
Hearty Smoked Meat Sandwiches, 22
Peppers with Smoked Fish Stuffing, 125
Smoked Chicken and Sweetbread Salad, 67
Smoked Chicken Liver and Shrimp, 213
Smoked Fish and Chili Mold, 166
Smoked Fish Louis, 154
Smoked Fish Luncheon Molds, 160
Smoked Liverwurst spread, 214
Smoked Shrimp Salad Supreme, 151
Smoked Turkey Club Sandwiches, 75

CHINESE CABBAGE:
Smoked Fish Chop Chop, 127

CHINESE NOODLES:
Smoked Rabbit Oriental, 93

CHINESE PEA PODS, FROZEN:
Smoked Fish Chop Chop, 127

CHINESE VEGETABLES, CANNED:
Smoked Beef Chop Suey for a Party, 14
Smoked Turkey Chow Mein, 45

CHIVES:
Chive Butter, 215
Cold Smoked Fish Soup, 133
Cottage Cheese Filling, 192
Scrambled Eggs and Smoked Fish on Toast, 142
Smoked Beef Salad, 19
Smoked Fish and Egg Spread, 170
Smoked Fish and Potato Salad, 165
Smoked Fish Mold Parisienne, 150
Smoked Shrimp Omelet Sandwich, 168
Smoked Squirrel Salad, 102
Smoked Turkey with Wild Rice, 28
Smoked Venison Surprise Salad, 106
Sweet and Sour Dressing, 150

CHOW MEIN NOODLES:
Chinese Smoked Chicken, 43
Lobster and Smoked Chicken Cantonese, 44
Smoked Chicken Chow Bake, 37
Smoked Chicken Chow Mein, 44
Smoked Fish Chow Mein, 126
Smoked Turkey Chow Mein, 45

CLAM JUICE:
Smoked Octopus Chowder, 132

CLOVES:
Apples with Smoked Chicken Stuffing, 80
Creole of Smoked Rabbit, 110
Japanese Mandarin Smoked Fish Loaf, 119
Smoked Rabbit Supreme, 94
Smoked Sausage, Apple and Yam Casserole, 181
Smoked Sausage with Sauerkraut, 183
Smoked Squirrel Far East, 93

COCKTAIL SAUCE:
California Smoked Shrimp Cocktail Sauce, 198

COCONUT:
Curried Smoked Chicken Salad, 63
Hawaiian Smoked Turkey, 59
Smoked Shrimp Tahiti, 144
Smoked Summer Sausage Tropical Salad, 186

COGNAC:
Pears and and Apples with Smoked Cheese Dip, 203
Smoked Octopus Chowder, 132
Smoked Venison Pâté, 196

CONSOMMÉ:
Creole of Smoked Rabbit, 110
Curried Smoked Fish, 145
Smoked Turkey and Tomato Mold, 72

CORN:
Corn and Smoked Beef Medley, 17
Fancy Smoked Fish Chowder, 132
Smoked Chicken and Corn Salad, 66
Smoked Chicken Tamale Pie, 30
Smoked Chipped Beef and Corn Casserole, 12
Smoked Rabbit Stew, 109
Smoked Venison One-Dish Meal, 85

CORN BREAD:
Quick-on-the-Draw Smoked Elk Curry, 95
Smoked Squirrel Supreme, 96
Smoked Turkey Supreme on Corn Bread, 66

CORN BREAD MIX:
Smoked Rabbit Almandine, 97
Southern Smoked Squirrel, 90

CORN CHIPS:
Hot Smoked Turkey Salad, 41
Smoked Venison and Noodles, 84

CORNMEAL:
Smoked Chicken Tamale Pie, 30
Smoked Fish Fritters, 141
Smoked Rabbit Tamale Pie, 86

COTTAGE CHEESE:
Cottage Cheese Filling, 192
Smoked Chicken Canapés, 190
Smoked Fish and Cottage Cheese Supreme, 117
Smoked Sausage Lasagne, 181

CRACKERS:
Lemony Smoked Fish Patties, 147
Peppers with Smoked Fish Stuffing, 125
Smoked Fish Patties, 147
Smoked Venison Loaf, 87

CRANBERRIES:
Avocado Filled with Smoked Fish, 148

CRANBERRY SAUCE:
Smoked Chicken Rolls, 51
Smoked Turkey Cranberry Mold, 64

CREAM:
California Smoked Shrimp Cocktail, 198
Chicken or Turkey Tetrazzini, 35
Chinese Smoked Chicken, 43
Creamed Smoked Chicken, 48
Creamed Smoked Chipped Beef, 15
Creamed Smoked Rabbit, 95
Crunchy Smoked Fish Salad, 154
Lemony Smoked Fish Crepes, 140
Pears and Apples with Smoked Cheese Dip, 203
Quick-on-the-Draw Smoked Elk Curry, 95
Scrambled Eggs and Smoked Fish on Toast, 142
Smoked Chicken à la King with Mushrooms, 48
Smoked Chicken Curry, 59
Smoked Chicken Hashed in Cream, 56
Smoked Chicken Liver and Anchovy Paste, 80
Smoked Chicken or Turkey and Rice Curry, 28
Smoked Chicken Ring or Loaf, 40

Smoked Chicken with Nuts and Spaghetti, 28
Smoked Fish au Gratin, 114
Smoked Fish Bisque, Continental Style, 131
Smoked Fish Salad with Roquefort, 152
Smoked Fish Soup, 133
Smoked Octopus Chowder, 132
Smoked Seafood Bisque, 130
Smoked Shrimp Casserole, 121
Smoked Shrimp Newburg, 136
Smoked Shrimp Salad, 163
Smoked Squirrel Almandine, 96
Smoked Squirrel Pie with Curried Potatoes, 90
Smoked Squirrel Supreme, 96
Smoked Turkey Hash, 56
Sweet Pickle and Smoked Poultry, 211

CREAM, HALF-AND-HALF:
Creamed Eggs in Smoked Fish Crust, 136
Peppered Smoked Fish and Eggs, 142
Smoked Chicken Liver Filling, 75
Smoked Fish Loaf with Noodles, 126
Smoked Fish Zarzuela, 143
Smoked Oyster Stew, 134
Smoked Rabbit Supreme, 94
Smoked Salmon Pensacola, 139
Smoked Sausage Potato Salad, 186

CREAM, WHIPPING:
Curried Venison, Seattle Style, 94
German Chicken Salad, 62
Imperial Gourmet Pie, 185
Smoked Chicken Almandine, 27
Smoked Chicken and Lobster Casserole, 37
Smoked Chicken Liver Spread or Filling, 191
Smoked Chicken Salad Mold, 72
Smoked Fish and Cucumber Mousse, 153
Smoked Fish Mousse, 153
Smoked Salmon Mousse with Horseradish, 157
Smoked Salmon Mousse with Mustard, 164
Smoked Shrimp Bisque, 130
Smoked Turkey or Chicken for a Party, 31
Smoked Turkey with Wild Rice, 28
Tangy Dressing, 20

CREAM CHEESE:
Celery Stuffed with Smoked Fish, 197
Deluxe Smoked Venison Sandwiches, 108
Dinty Moore Celery Sticks, 189
Rolled Hors d'Oeuvres, 189
Sandwich Loaf, 195
Sandwich Loaves, 192
Smoked Clam Appetizer Dip, 200
Smoked Clam Spread, 206
Smoked Dried Beef Rolls, 188
Smoked Fish and Cheese Dip, 200
Smoked Fish and Tomato Mold, 152
Smoked Fish Dip, 201
Smoked Liver Sausage, 214
Smoked Moss Balls, 204
Smoked Oyster Dip, 200
Smoked Salmon and Celery Rolls, 201
Smoked Shrimp Salad Sandwich, 175
Smoked Venison Rolls, 197

CROUTONS, HERB-SEASONED:
Smoked Fish Loaf with Sour Cream, 123

CUCUMBER:
Chef's Salad Bowl, 74
Cold Smoked Fish Soup, 133
Jellied Smoked Fish Mold, 155
Molded Smoked Fish and Potato Salad, 165
Molded Smoked Turkey Salad, 62
Open Face Broiled Smoked Fish Sandwich, 169
Smoked Clam Spread, 206

Where to Find Types of Dishes